ATLAS OF THE HUMAN BODY

Frederic H. Martini, Ph.D.
University of Hawaii

Michael J. Timmons, M.S.
Moraine Valley Community College

Robert B. Tallitsch, Ph.D.
Augustana College

Ralph T. Hutchings
Biomedical Photographer

PEARSON

Benjamin
Cummings

Library of Congress Cataloging-in-Publication Data

Martini, Frederic.
    Atlas of the human body to accompany Human Anatomy, 4th ed. / Frederic H. Martini,
Michael J. Timmons, Robert B. Tallitsch, with William C. Ober … [et al.].
        p. cm.
    ISBN 0-13-008906-0
    1. Human anatomy--Atlases.   I. Timmons, Michael J.   II. Tallitsch, Robert B.
    III. Martini, Frederic.   IV. Title.

QM23.2.M356 2003 Suppl.
611'.0022'3—dc21

2002030721

Prentice Hall
Senior Editor: Halee Dinsey
Production Editor: Prepare, Inc.
Executive Managing Editor: Kathleen Schiaparelli
Assistant Managing Editor: Beth Sweeten
AV Editor: Adam Velthaus
Art Studio: Patty Gutierrez
Cover Designer: Alamini Design
Cover Illustration: Vincent Perez
Manufacturing Manager: Trudy Pisciotti
Manufacturing Buyer: Alan Fischer
Vice President of Production and Manufacturing: David W. Riccardi

Benjamin Cummings
Publisher: Daryl Fox
Executive Editor: Leslie Berriman
Development Manager: Claire Brassert
Associate Editor: Nicole George
Editorial Assistant: Michael Roney
Executive Producer: Lauren Fogel
Associate Media Project Editor: Kim Neumann
Managing Editor: Deborah Cogan
Manufacturing Buyer: Stacey Weinberger
Executive Marketing Manager: Lauren Harp

Notice: Our knowledge in clinical sciences is constantly changing. The author and the publisher of this volume have taken care that the information contained herein is accurate and compatible with the standards generally accepted at the time of publication. Nevertheless, it is difficult to ensure that all information given is entirely accurate for all circumstances. The author and the publisher disclaim any liability, loss, or damage incurred as a consequence, directly or indirectly, of the use and application of any of the contents of this volume.

Printed in the United States of America
10 9 8 7 6 5 4 3 2 1

ISBN 0-13-008906-0

Pearson Education LTD., *London*
Pearson Education Australia PTY, Limited, *Sydney*
Pearson Education Singapore, Pte. Ltd
Pearson Education North Asia Ltd, *Hong Kong*
Pearson Education Canada, Ltd., *Toronto*
Pearson Educación de Mexico, *S.A. de C.V.*
Pearson Education—Japan, *Tokyo*
Pearson Education Malaysia, Pte. Ltd

PEARSON
Benjamin Cummings

CONTENTS

ILLUSTRATION CREDITS

Scans

1a-e, 2a-d, 3a-b, 4, 5a-b, 6a-b, 7a-b, 8a-b, 9a-f, 9g-i — Courtesy of Dr. Eugene C. Wasson, III, and staff of Maui Radiology Consultants, Maui Memorial Hospital

10a-b, d — Picker International

10c — Kathleen Welch, M.D.

Bones

1, 2, 3.1-3.3, 3.4, 4.1- 4.3, 5.1-5.5, 6.1-6.4b, 6.5a, 6.6-6.8a, 6.9a-6.18, 7.1-7.3, 7.5a-f, 8.1- 8.4, 8.6-8.19, 9.1-9.11 — Ralph T. Hutchings

4.2 — Michael J. Timmons

8.3 — Bates/Custom Medical Stock Photo, Inc.

Cadavers

1.1, 1.2, 1.4, 1.5, 2.1, 2.2, 3.1, 3.2, 4.1, 4.2a-b, 4.3a-b, 5.1, 5.2, 5.2b, 5.3a-d, 5.4a-d, 5.5, 5.6a-b, 5.7a-b, 5.8a-b, 5.9, 5.10a-b, 6.1, 6.2, 6.3, 6.4a, 6.4b — Ralph T. Hutchings

6.6a, 8.12d, 6.5c — Patrick M. Timmons/Michael J. Timmons

1.3 — University of Toronto

Histology

All histology images courtesy of Robert B. Tallitsch, Ph.D. with Ronald Guastaferri, B.A., M.A.M.S.

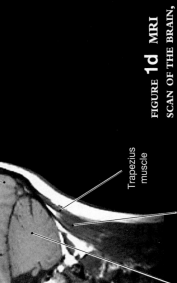

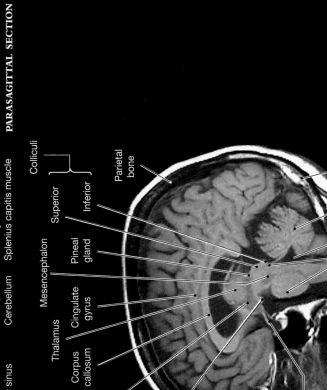

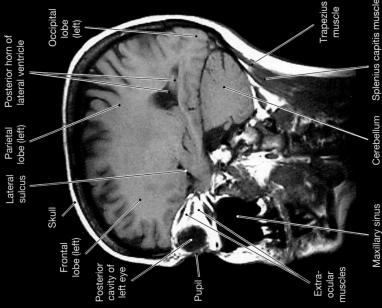

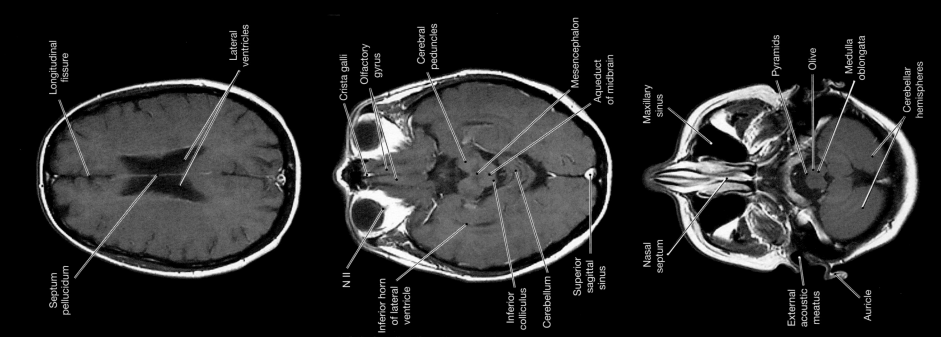

FIGURE 1d MRI
SCAN OF THE BRAIN,
PARASAGITTAL SECTION

FIGURE 1e MRI
SCAN OF THE BRAIN,
MIDSAGITTAL SECTION

FIGURE 1a MRI
SCAN OF THE BRAIN,
HORIZONTAL SECTION

FIGURE 1b MRI
SCAN OF THE BRAIN,
HORIZONTAL SECTION

FIGURE 1c MRI
SCAN OF THE BRAIN,
HORIZONTAL SECTION

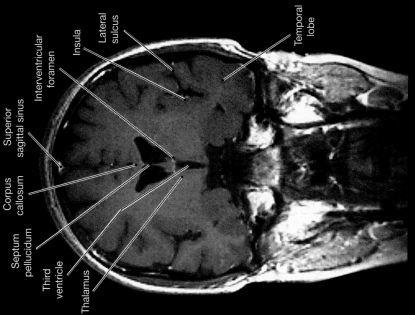

FIGURE **2a** MRI
SCAN OF THE BRAIN,
CORONAL SECTION

Longitudinal fissure

Lateral ventricle

Left frontal lobe

Temporal lobe

Inferior nasal concha

Masseter muscle

Sphenoidal sinus

Nasal septum

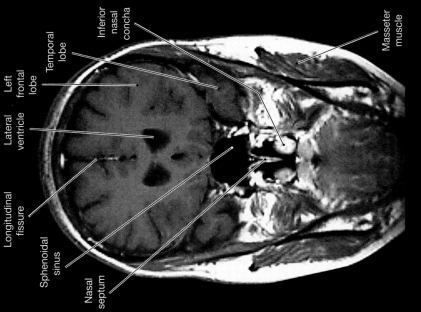

FIGURE **2c** MRI
SCAN OF THE BRAIN,
CORONAL SECTION

Superior sagittal sinus

Corpus callosum

Longitudinal fissure

Choroid plexus

Lateral ventricle

Mesencephalon

Temporal lobe

Septum pellucidum

Third ventricle

Thalamus

Pons

Medulla oblongata

Cerebellar peduncles

Spinal cord

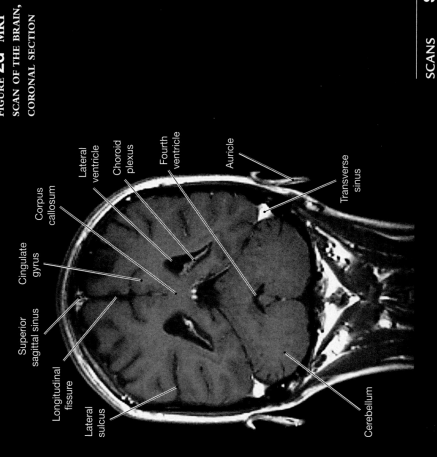

FIGURE **2b** MRI
SCAN OF THE BRAIN,
CORONAL SECTION

Superior sagittal sinus

Corpus callosum

Interventricular foramen

Insula

Lateral sulcus

Septum pellucidum

Third ventricle

Thalamus

Temporal lobe

Superior sagittal sinus

Cingulate gyrus

Corpus callosum

Lateral ventricle

Choroid plexus

Fourth ventricle

Auricle

Longitudinal fissure

Lateral sulcus

Transverse sinus

Cerebellum

FIGURE **2d** MRI
SCAN OF THE BRAIN,
CORONAL SECTION

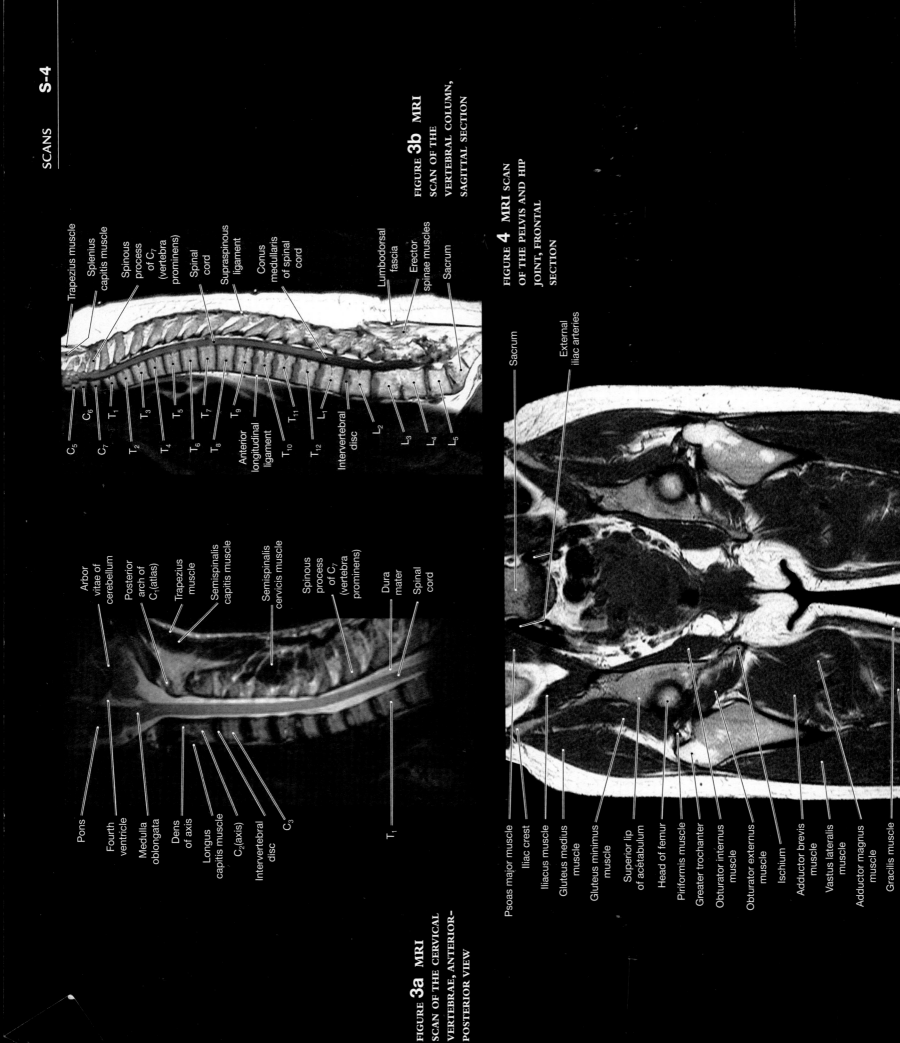

FIGURE **3a** MRI
SCAN OF THE CERVICAL
VERTEBRAE, ANTERIOR-
POSTERIOR VIEW

- Pons
- Fourth ventricle
- Medulla oblongata
- Dens of axis
- Longus capitis muscle
- C₂(axis)
- Intervertebral disc
- C₃
- T₁

- Arbor vitae of cerebellum
- Posterior arch of C₁(atlas)
- Trapezius muscle
- Semispinalis capitis muscle
- Semispinalis cervicis muscle
- Spinous process of C₇ (vertebra prominens)
- Dura mater
- Spinal cord

FIGURE **3b** MRI
SCAN OF THE
VERTEBRAL COLUMN,
SAGITTAL SECTION

- Trapezius muscle
- Splenius capitis muscle
- Spinous process of C₇ (vertebra prominens)
- Spinal cord
- Supraspinous ligament
- Conus medullaris of spinal cord
- Lumbodorsal fascia
- Erector spinae muscles
- Sacrum

- C₅
- C₆
- C₇
- T₁
- T₂
- T₃
- T₄
- T₅
- T₆
- T₇
- T₈
- T₉
- Anterior longitudinal ligament
- T₁₀
- T₁₁
- T₁₂
- L₁
- Intervertebral disc
- L₂
- L₃
- L₄
- L₅

FIGURE **4** MRI SCAN
OF THE PELVIS AND HIP
JOINT, FRONTAL
SECTION

- Sacrum
- External iliac arteries
- Psoas major muscle
- Iliac crest
- Iliacus muscle
- Gluteus medius muscle
- Gluteus minimus muscle
- Superior lip of acetabulum
- Head of femur
- Piriformis muscle
- Greater trochanter
- Obturator internus muscle
- Obturator externus muscle
- Ischium
- Adductor brevis muscle
- Vastus lateralis muscle
- Adductor magnus muscle
- Gracilis muscle
- Deep femoral artery
- Vastus intermedius muscle
- Biceps femoris muscle

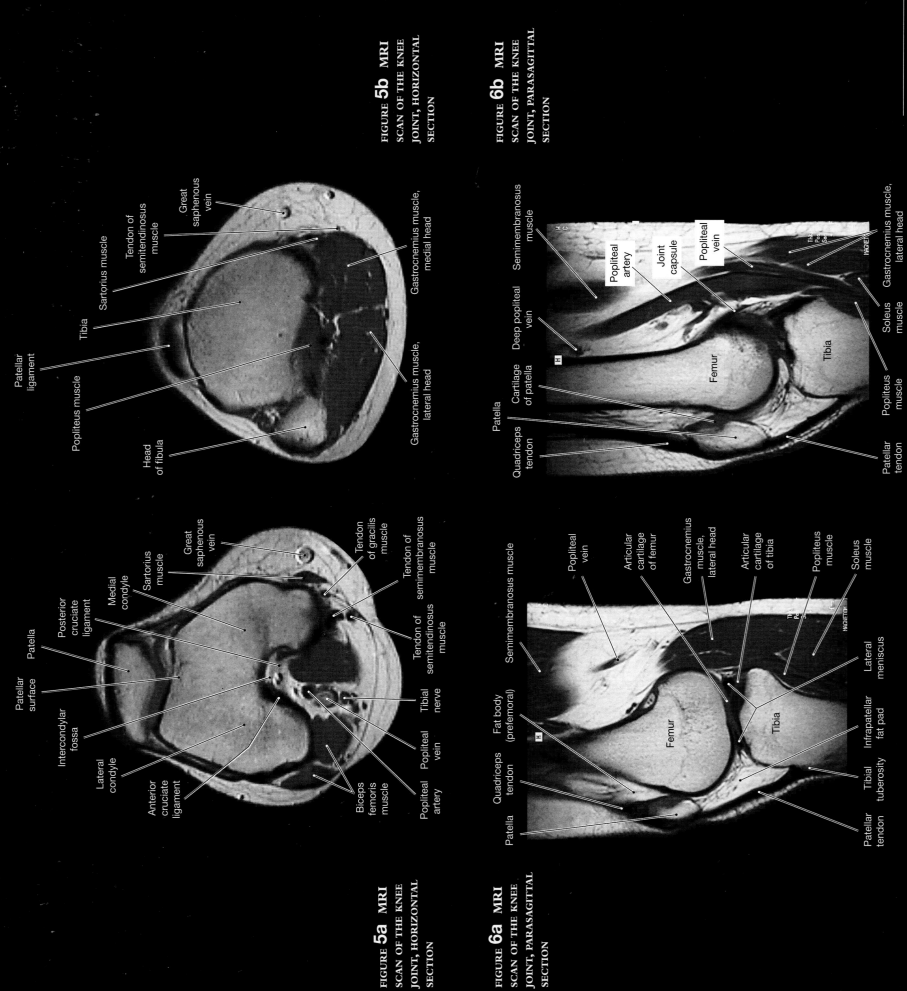

FIGURE 5a MRI SCAN OF THE KNEE JOINT, HORIZONTAL SECTION

Patellar surface
Patella
Posterior cruciate ligament
Medial condyle
Sartorius muscle
Great saphenous vein
Tendon of gracilis muscle
Tendon of semimembranosus muscle
Intercondylar fossa
Lateral condyle
Anterior cruciate ligament
Biceps femoris muscle
Popliteal vein
Popliteal artery
Tibial nerve
Tendon of semitendinosus muscle

FIGURE 5b MRI SCAN OF THE KNEE JOINT, HORIZONTAL SECTION

Patellar ligament
Tibia
Sartorius muscle
Tendon of semitendinosus muscle
Great saphenous vein
Popliteus muscle
Head of fibula
Gastrocnemius muscle, lateral head
Gastrocnemius muscle, medial head

FIGURE 6a MRI SCAN OF THE KNEE JOINT, PARASAGITTAL SECTION

Semimembranosus muscle
Popliteal vein
Articular cartilage of femur
Gastrocnemius muscle, lateral head
Articular cartilage of tibia
Popliteus muscle
Soleus muscle
Quadriceps tendon
Fat body (prefemoral)
Patella
Femur
Tibia
Lateral meniscus
Patellar tendon
Tibial tuberosity
Infrapatellar fat pad

FIGURE 6b MRI SCAN OF THE KNEE JOINT, PARASAGITTAL SECTION

Semimembranosus muscle
Popliteal artery
Joint capsule
Popliteal vein
Gastrocnemius muscle, lateral head
Deep popliteal vein
Cartilage of patella
Patella
Quadriceps tendon
Femur
Tibia
Soleus muscle
Popliteus muscle
Patellar tendon

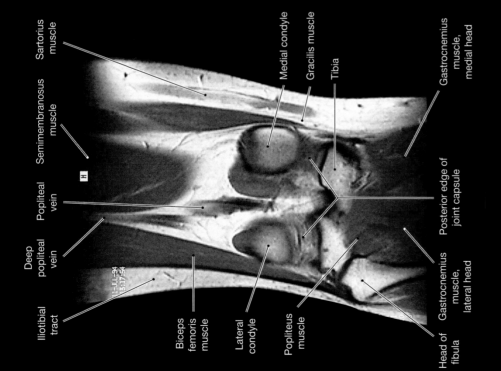
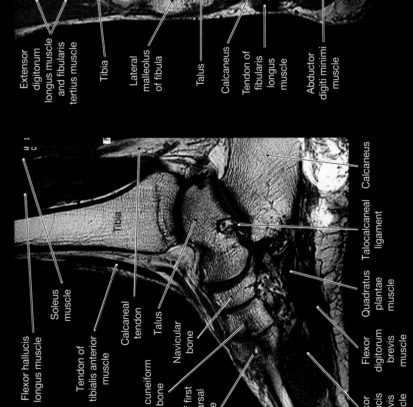

Posterior cruciate ligament
Vastus medialis muscle
Medial condyle of femur
Medial meniscus
Tibial collateral ligament
Great saphenous vein
Intercondylar fossa
Gastrocnemius muscle, medial head
Popliteal vein
Tibia
Biceps femoris muscle
Epiphyseal line
Anterior cruciate ligament
Lateral condyle of femur
Fibular collateral ligament
Lateral meniscus
Tubercles of intercondylar eminence of tibia

FIGURE **7b** MRI SCAN OF THE KNEE JOINT, FRONTAL SECTION

Medial malleolus of tibia
Tendon of tibialis posterior muscle
Deltoid ligament
Tendon of flexor digitorum longus muscle
Tendon of flexor hallucis longus muscle
Plantar artery
Abductor hallucis muscle
Quadratus plantae muscle
Flexor digitorum brevis muscle
Extensor digitorum longus muscle and fibularis tertius muscle
Tibia
Lateral malleolus of fibula
Talus
Calcaneus
Tendon of fibularis longus muscle
Abductor digiti minimi muscle

FIGURE **8b** MRI SCAN OF THE ANKLE JOINT, FRONTAL SECTION

Sartorius muscle
Semimembranosus muscle
Medial condyle
Gracilis muscle
Tibia
Popliteal vein
Deep popliteal vein
Gastrocnemius muscle, medial head
Iliotibial tract
Biceps femoris muscle
Lateral condyle
Popliteus muscle
Gastrocnemius muscle, lateral head
Head of fibula
Posterior edge of joint capsule

FIGURE **7a** MRI SCAN OF THE KNEE JOINT, FRONTAL SECTION

Flexor hallucis longus muscle
Soleus muscle
Calcaneal tendon
Talus
Tibia
Calcaneus
Tendon of tibialis anterior muscle
Navicular bone
First cuneiform bone
Head of first metatarsal bone
Flexor hallucis brevis muscle
Flexor digitorum brevis muscle
Quadratus plantae muscle
Talocalcaneal ligament

FIGURE **8a** MRI SCAN OF THE ANKLE JOINT, PARASAGITTAL SECTION

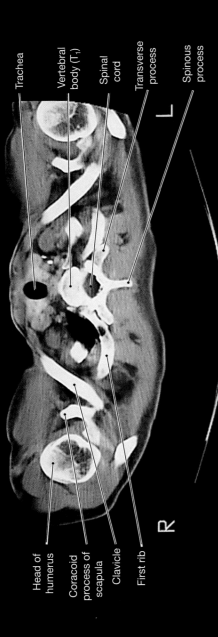

FIGURE 9a MRI
SCAN OF THE TRUNK,
HORIZONTAL SECTION

Trachea
Vertebral body (T₁)
Spinal cord
Transverse process
Spinous process
Head of humerus
Coracoid process of scapula
Clavicle
First rib
L
R

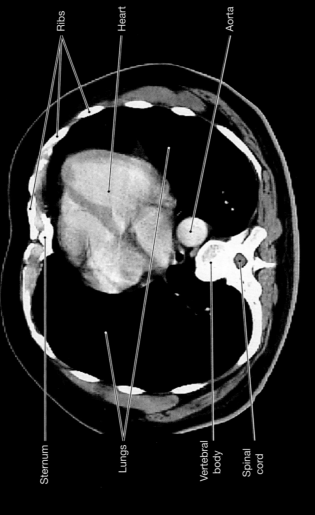

FIGURE 9b MRI
SCAN OF THE TRUNK,
HORIZONTAL SECTION

Ribs
Heart
Aorta
Sternum
Lungs
Vertebral body
Spinal cord

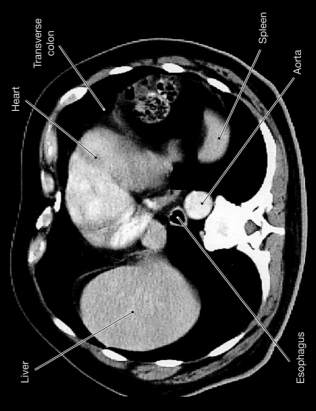

FIGURE 9c MRI
SCAN OF THE TRUNK,
HORIZONTAL SECTION

Heart
Transverse colon
Spleen
Aorta
Liver
Esophagus

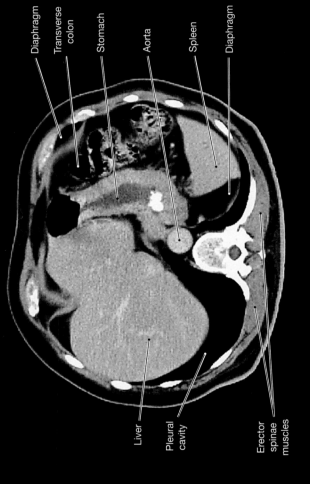

FIGURE **9d** MRI
SCAN OF THE TRUNK,
HORIZONTAL SECTION

Diaphragm
Transverse colon
Stomach
Aorta
Spleen
Diaphragm
Liver
Pleural cavity
Erector spinae muscles

FIGURE **9e** MRI
SCAN OF THE TRUNK,
HORIZONTAL SECTION

Transverse colon
Small intestine
Aorta
Spleen
Left kidney
Transverse colon
Liver
Right kidney
Diaghragm

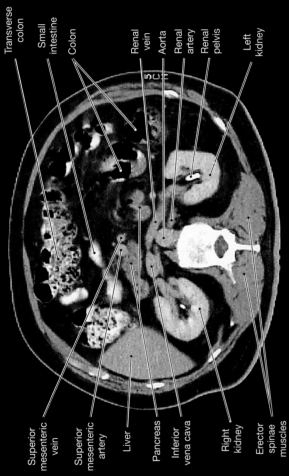

FIGURE **9f** MRI SCAN
OF THE TRUNK,
HORIZONTAL SECTION

Transverse colon
Small intestine
Colon
Renal vein
Aorta
Renal artery
Renal pelvis
Left kidney
Superior mesenteric vein
Superior mesenteric artery
Liver
Pancreas
Inferior vena cava
Right kidney
Erector spinae muscles

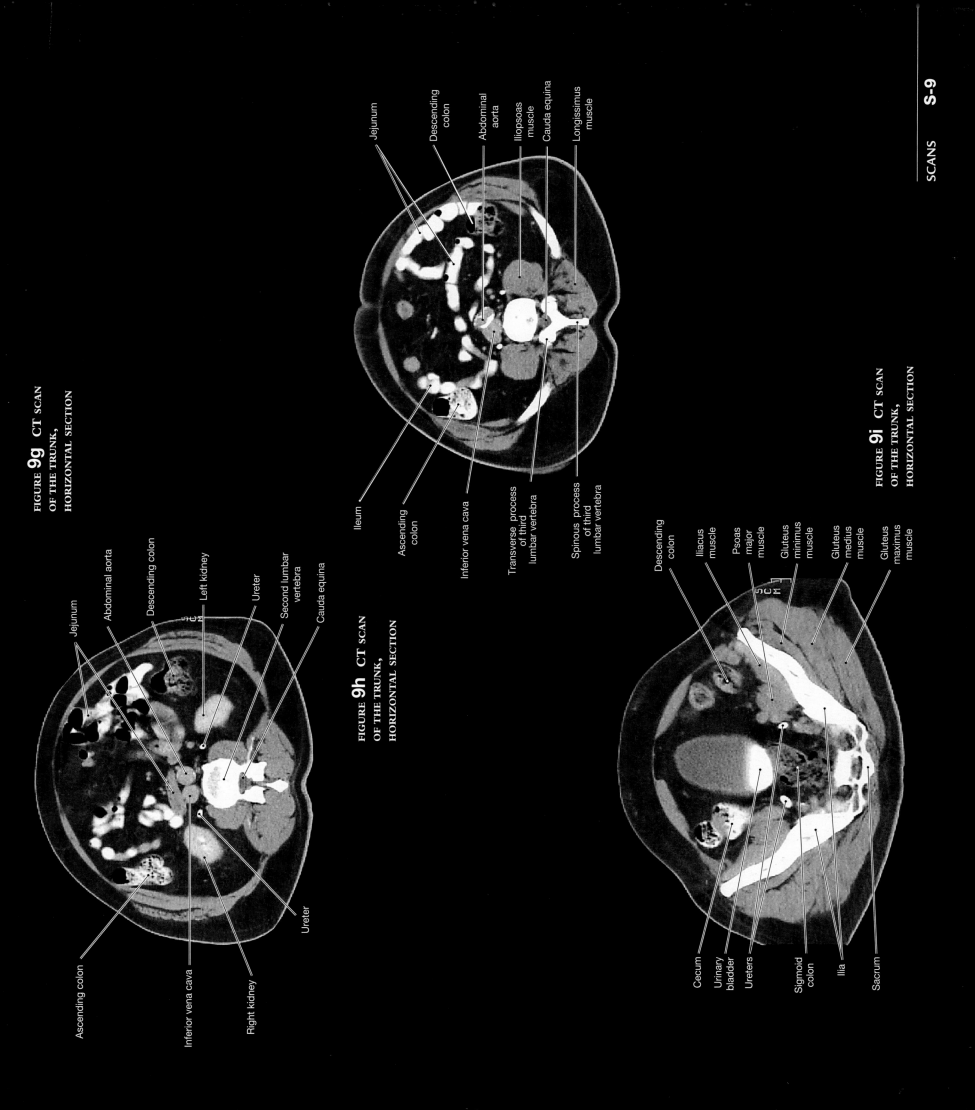

FIGURE 9g CT SCAN OF THE TRUNK, HORIZONTAL SECTION

- Jejunum
- Abdominal aorta
- Descending colon
- Left kidney
- Ureter
- Second lumbar vertebra
- Cauda equina
- Ascending colon
- Inferior vena cava
- Right kidney
- Ureter

FIGURE 9h CT SCAN OF THE TRUNK, HORIZONTAL SECTION

- Jejunum
- Descending colon
- Abdominal aorta
- Iliopsoas muscle
- Cauda equina
- Longissimus muscle
- Ileum
- Ascending colon
- Inferior vena cava
- Transverse process of third lumbar vertebra
- Spinous process of third lumbar vertebra

FIGURE 9i CT SCAN OF THE TRUNK, HORIZONTAL SECTION

- Descending colon
- Iliacus muscle
- Psoas major muscle
- Gluteus minimus muscle
- Gluteus medius muscle
- Gluteus maximus muscle
- Cecum
- Urinary bladder
- Ureters
- Sigmoid colon
- Ilia
- Sacrum

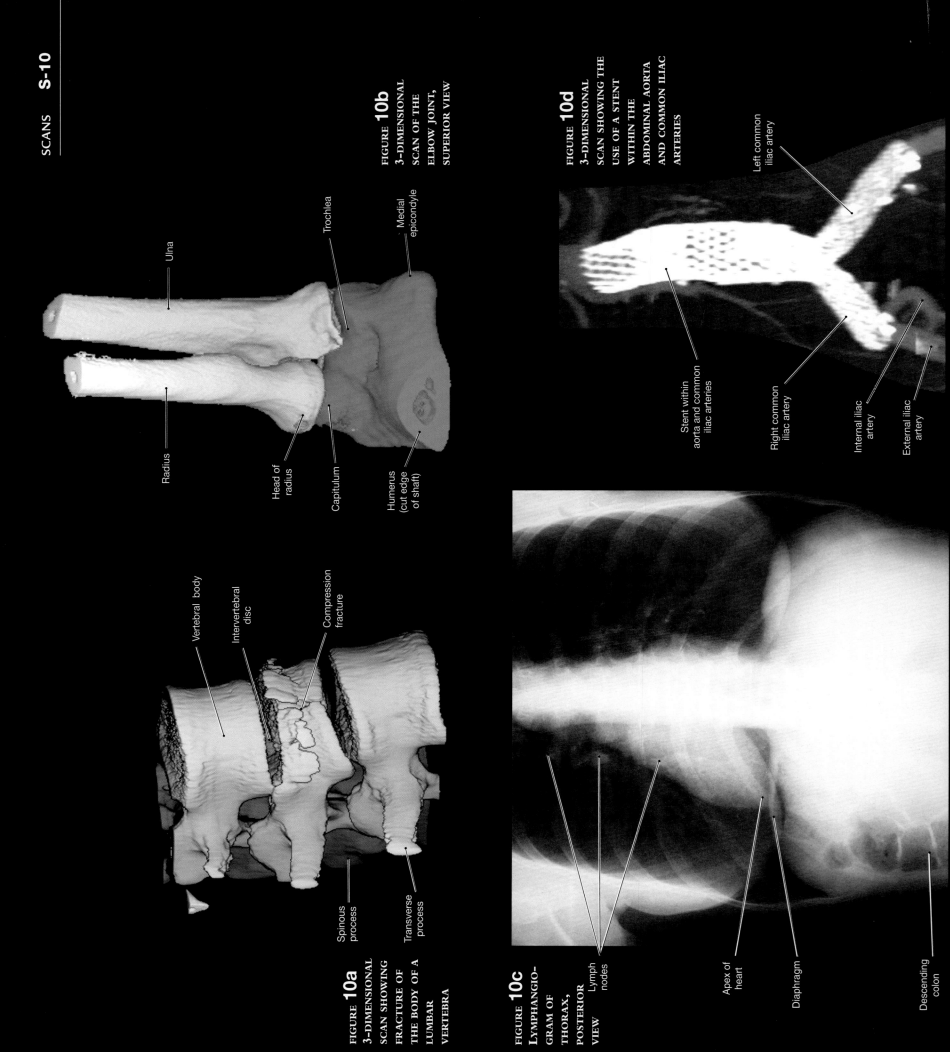

FIGURE **10a**
3–DIMENSIONAL
SCAN SHOWING
FRACTURE OF
THE BODY OF A
LUMBAR
VERTEBRA

Vertebral body

Intervertebral disc

Compression fracture

Spinous process

Transverse process

FIGURE **10b**
3–DIMENSIONAL
SCAN OF THE
ELBOW JOINT,
SUPERIOR VIEW

Ulna

Radius

Trochlea

Head of radius

Capitulum

Medial epicondyle

Humerus (cut edge of shaft)

FIGURE **10c**
LYMPHANGIO–
GRAM OF
THORAX,
POSTERIOR
VIEW

Lymph nodes

Apex of heart

Diaphragm

Descending colon

FIGURE **10d**
3–DIMENSIONAL
SCAN SHOWING THE
USE OF A STENT
WITHIN THE
ABDOMINAL AORTA
AND COMMON ILIAC
ARTERIES

Left common iliac artery

Stent within aorta and common iliac arteries

Right common iliac artery

Internal iliac artery

External iliac artery

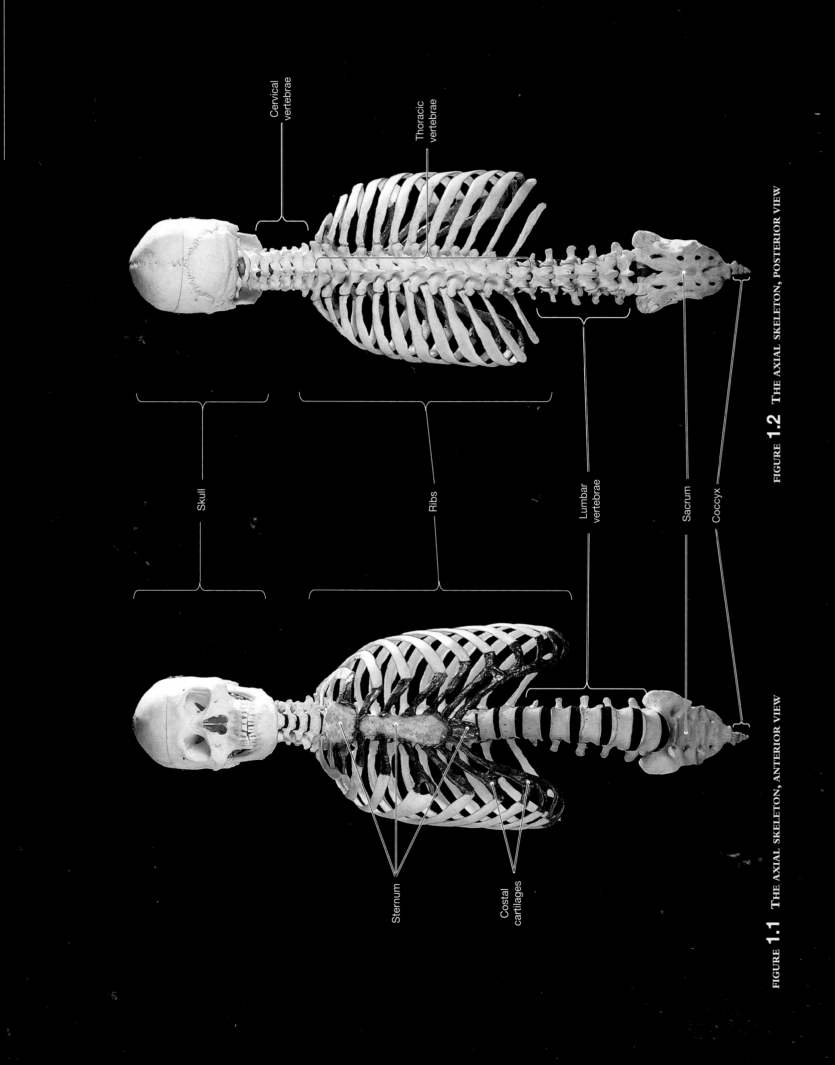

Cervical vertebrae

Thoracic vertebrae

Skull

Ribs

Lumbar vertebrae

Sacrum

Coccyx

Sternum

Costal cartilages

FIGURE **1.2** THE AXIAL SKELETON, POSTERIOR VIEW

FIGURE **1.1** THE AXIAL SKELETON, ANTERIOR VIEW

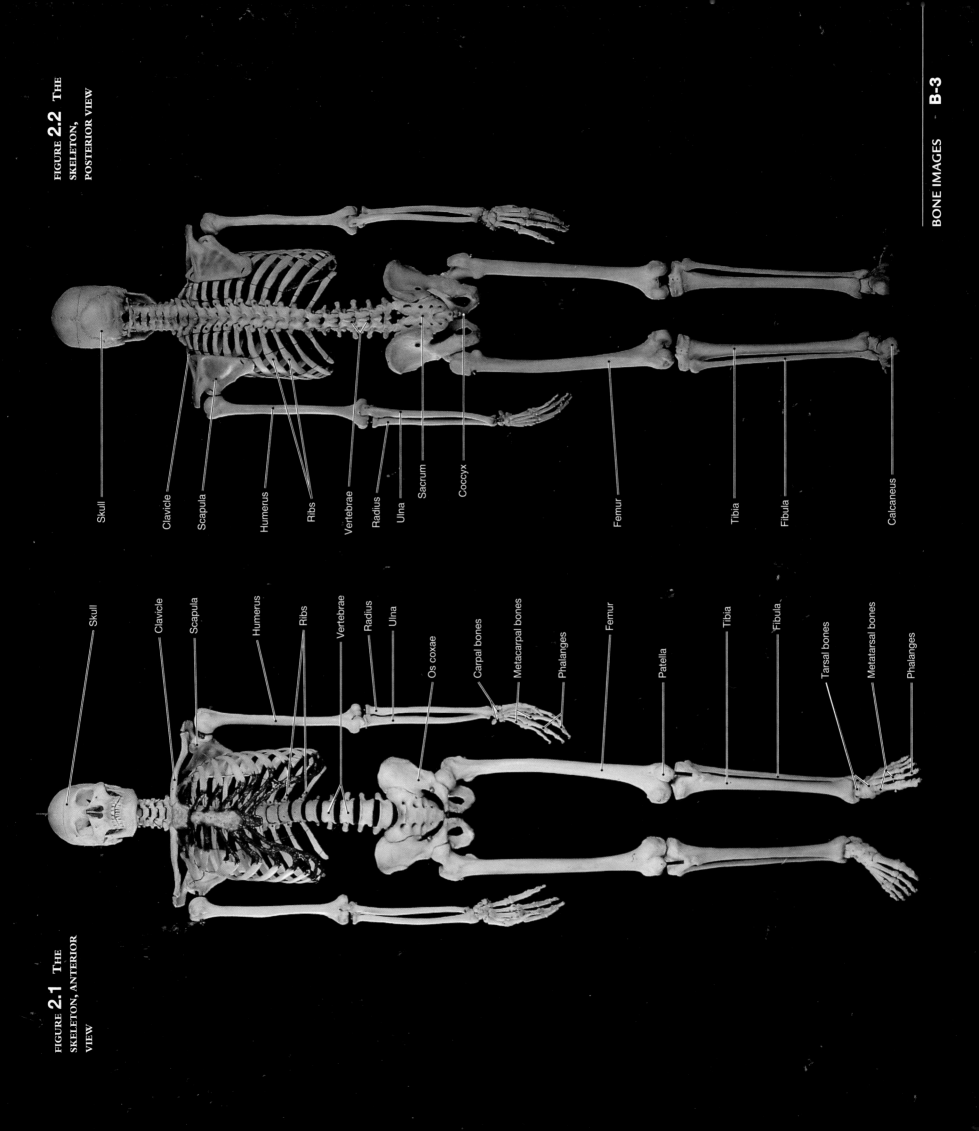

FIGURE **2.2** THE SKELETON, POSTERIOR VIEW

Skull

Clavicle

Scapula

Humerus

Ribs

Vertebrae

Radius

Ulna

Sacrum

Coccyx

Femur

Tibia

Fibula

Calcaneus

FIGURE **2.1** THE SKELETON, ANTERIOR VIEW

Skull

Clavicle

Scapula

Humerus

Ribs

Vertebrae

Radius

Ulna

Os coxae

Carpal bones

Metacarpal bones

Phalanges

Femur

Patella

Tibia

Fibula

Tarsal bones

Metatarsal bones

Phalanges

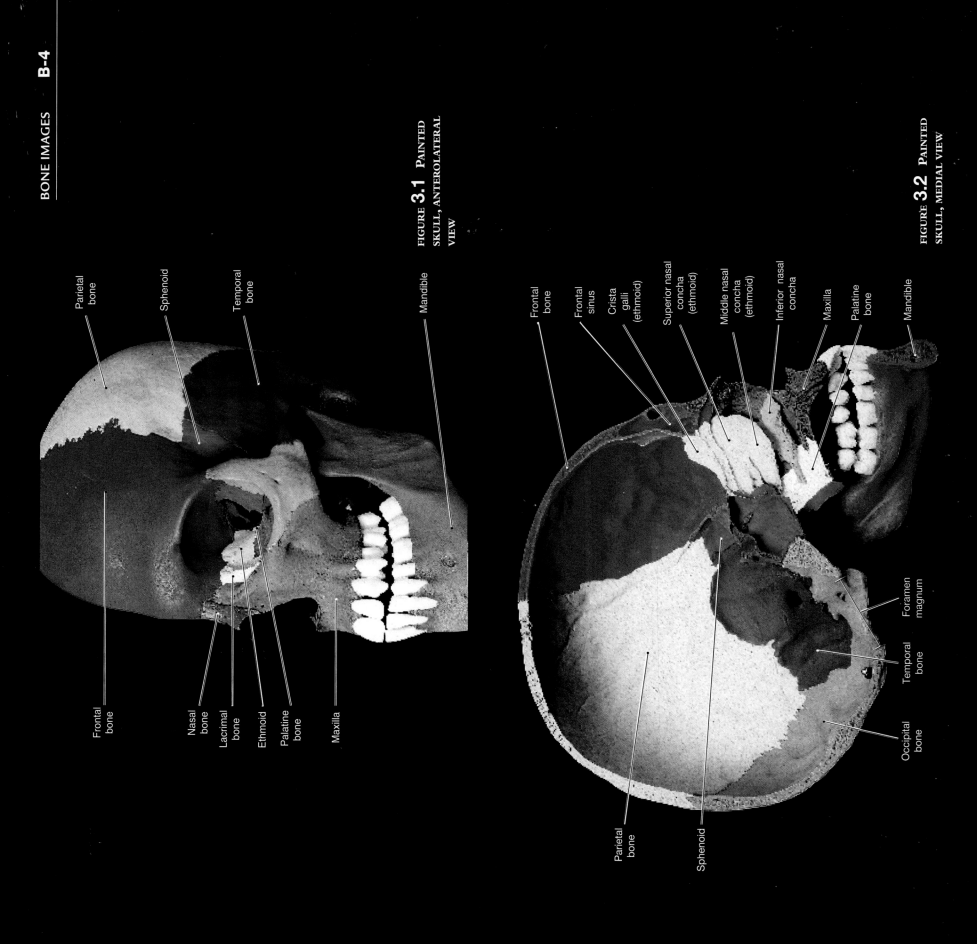

FIGURE 3.1 PAINTED SKULL, ANTEROLATERAL VIEW

Parietal bone
Sphenoid
Temporal bone
Mandible
Frontal bone
Nasal bone
Lacrimal bone
Ethmoid
Palatine bone
Maxilla

FIGURE 3.2 PAINTED SKULL, MEDIAL VIEW

Frontal bone
Frontal sinus
Crista galli (ethmoid)
Superior nasal concha (ethmoid)
Middle nasal concha (ethmoid)
Inferior nasal concha
Maxilla
Palatine bone
Mandible
Parietal bone
Sphenoid
Foramen magnum
Temporal bone
Occipital bone

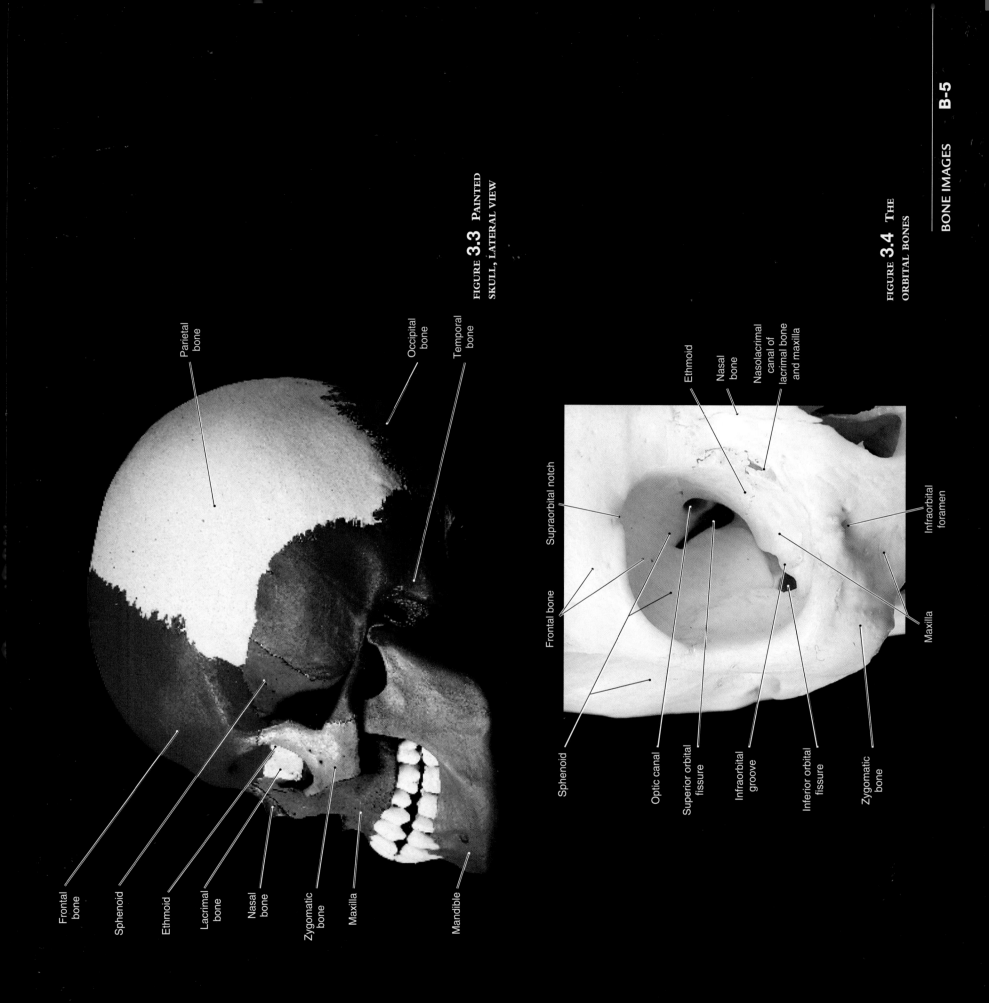

Parietal bone

Occipital bone

Temporal bone

Frontal bone

Sphenoid

Ethmoid

Lacrimal bone

Nasal bone

Zygomatic bone

Maxilla

Mandible

FIGURE 3.3 PAINTED SKULL, LATERAL VIEW

Ethmoid

Nasal bone

Nasolacrimal canal of lacrimal bone and maxilla

Supraorbital notch

Infraorbital foramen

Frontal bone

Sphenoid

Optic canal

Superior orbital fissure

Infraorbital groove

Inferior orbital fissure

Maxilla

Zygomatic bone

FIGURE 3.4 THE ORBITAL BONES

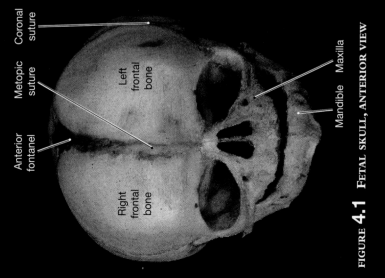

FIGURE **4.1** FETAL SKULL, ANTERIOR VIEW

Anterior fontanel
Metopic suture
Coronal suture
Left frontal bone
Right frontal bone
Mandible   Maxilla

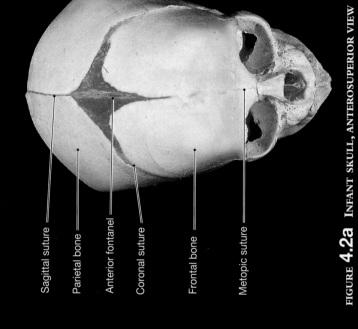

FIGURE **4.2a** INFANT SKULL, ANTEROSUPERIOR VIEW

Sagittal suture
Parietal bone
Anterior fontanel
Coronal suture
Frontal bone
Metopic suture

FIGURE **4.2b** INFANT SKULL, POSTERIOR VIEW

Sagittal suture
Parietal bone
Posterior fontanel
Lambdoid suture
Occipital bone

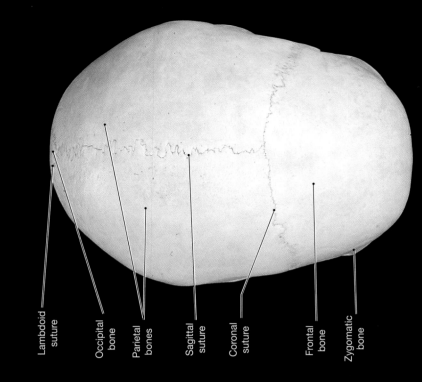

FIGURE **5.1b** ADULT SKULL, SUPERIOR VIEW

Lambdoid suture
Occipital bone
Parietal bones
Sagittal suture
Coronal suture
Frontal bone
Zygomatic bone

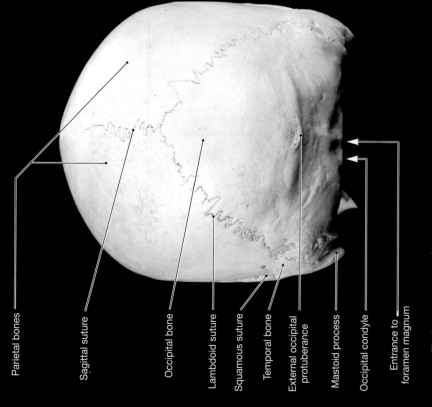

FIGURE **5.1a** ADULT SKULL, POSTERIOR VIEW

Parietal bones
Sagittal suture
Occipital bone
Lambdoid suture
Squamous suture
Temporal bone
External occipital protuberance
Mastoid process
Occipital condyle
Entrance to foramen magnum

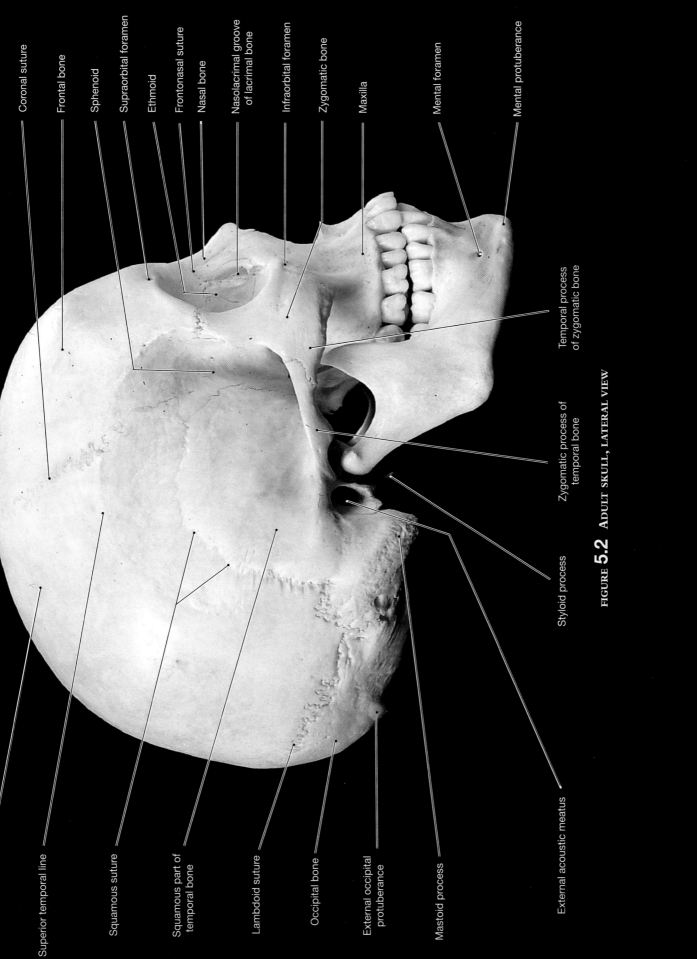

Coronal suture

Frontal bone

Sphenoid

Supraorbital foramen

Ethmoid

Frontonasal suture

Nasal bone

Nasolacrimal groove
of lacrimal bone

Infraorbital foramen

Zygomatic bone

Maxilla

Mental foramen

Mental protuberance

Parietal bone

Superior temporal line

Squamous suture

Squamous part of
temporal bone

Lambdoid suture

Occipital bone

External occipital
protuberance

Mastoid process

External acoustic meatus

Styloid process

Zygomatic process of
temporal bone

Temporal process
of zygomatic bone

FIGURE **5.2** ADULT SKULL, LATERAL VIEW

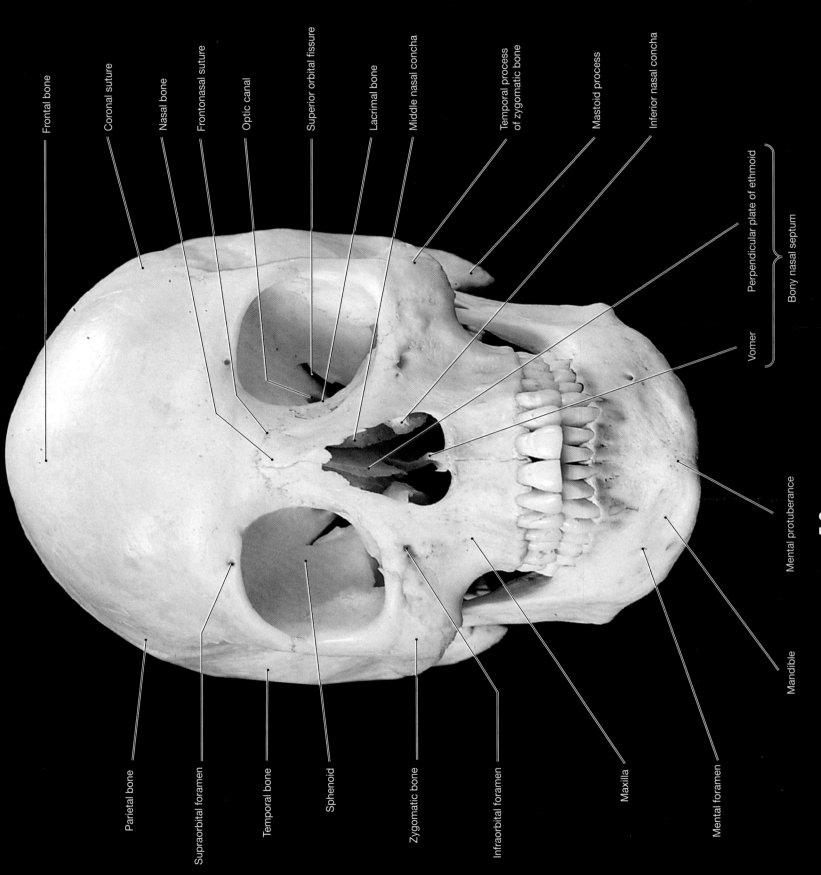

Frontal bone

Coronal suture

Nasal bone

Frontonasal suture

Optic canal

Superior orbital fissure

Lacrimal bone

Middle nasal concha

Temporal process of zygomatic bone

Mastoid process

Inferior nasal concha

Perpendicular plate of ethmoid

Vomer

Bony nasal septum

Parietal bone

Supraorbital foramen

Temporal bone

Sphenoid

Zygomatic bone

Infraorbital foramen

Maxilla

Mental foramen

Mandible

Mental protuberance

FIGURE **5.3** ADULT SKULL, ANTERIOR VIEW

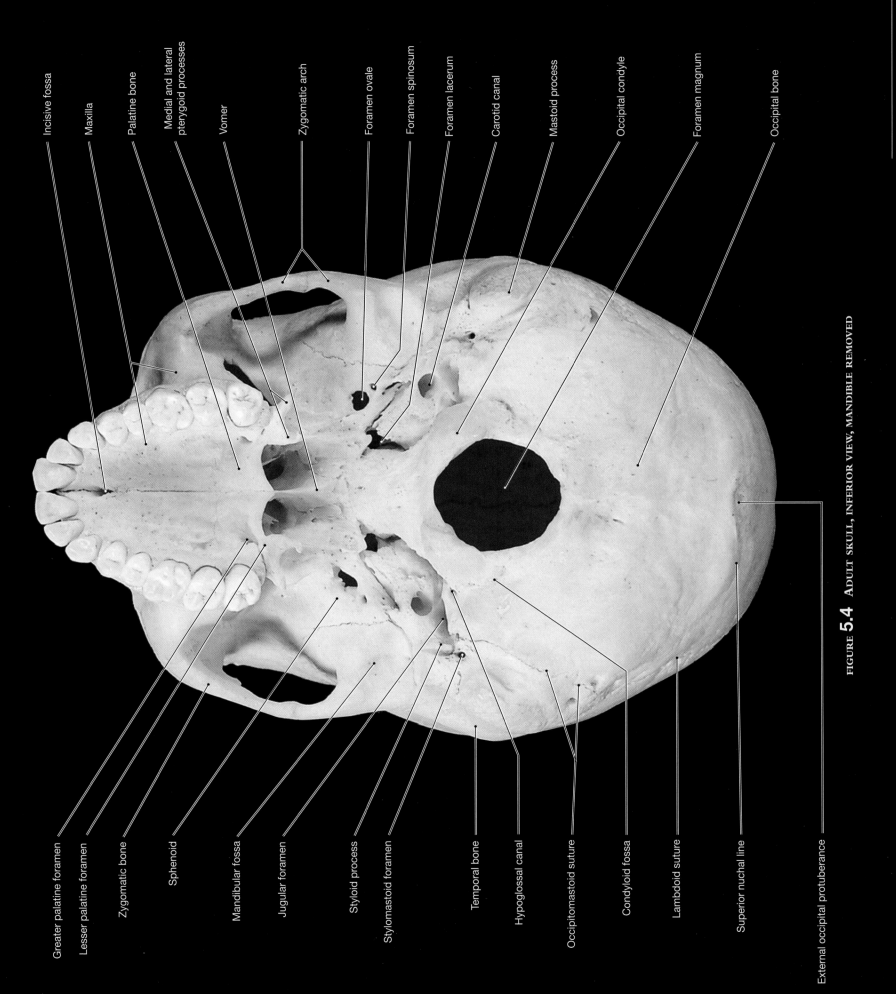

Incisive fossa

Maxilla

Palatine bone

Medial and lateral
pterygoid processes

Vomer

Zygomatic arch

Foramen ovale

Foramen spinosum

Foramen lacerum

Carotid canal

Mastoid process

Occipital condyle

Foramen magnum

Occipital bone

Greater palatine foramen

Lesser palatine foramen

Zygomatic bone

Sphenoid

Mandibular fossa

Jugular foramen

Styloid process

Stylomastoid foramen

Temporal bone

Hypoglossal canal

Occipitomastoid suture

Condyloid fossa

Lambdoid suture

Superior nuchal line

External occipital protuberance

FIGURE **5.4** ADULT SKULL, INFERIOR VIEW, MANDIBLE REMOVED

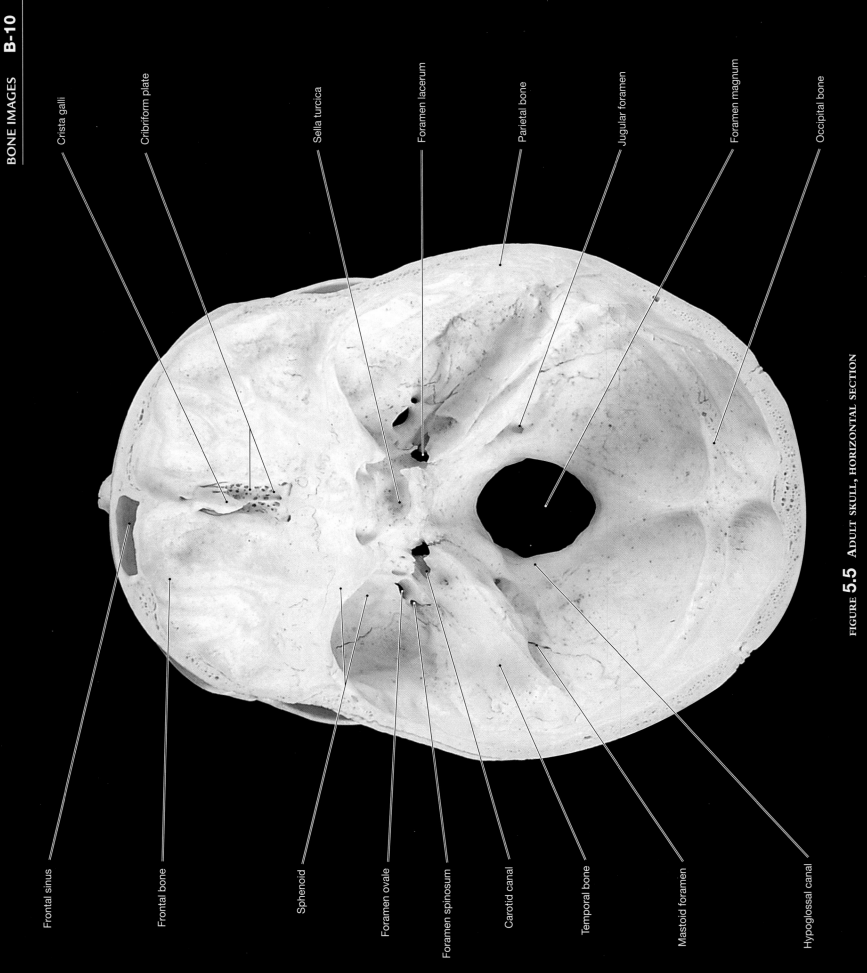

Crista galli

Cribriform plate

Sella turcica

Foramen lacerum

Parietal bone

Jugular foramen

Foramen magnum

Occipital bone

Frontal sinus

Frontal bone

Sphenoid

Foramen ovale

Foramen spinosum

Carotid canal

Temporal bone

Mastoid foramen

Hypoglossal canal

FIGURE 5.5 ADULT SKULL, HORIZONTAL SECTION

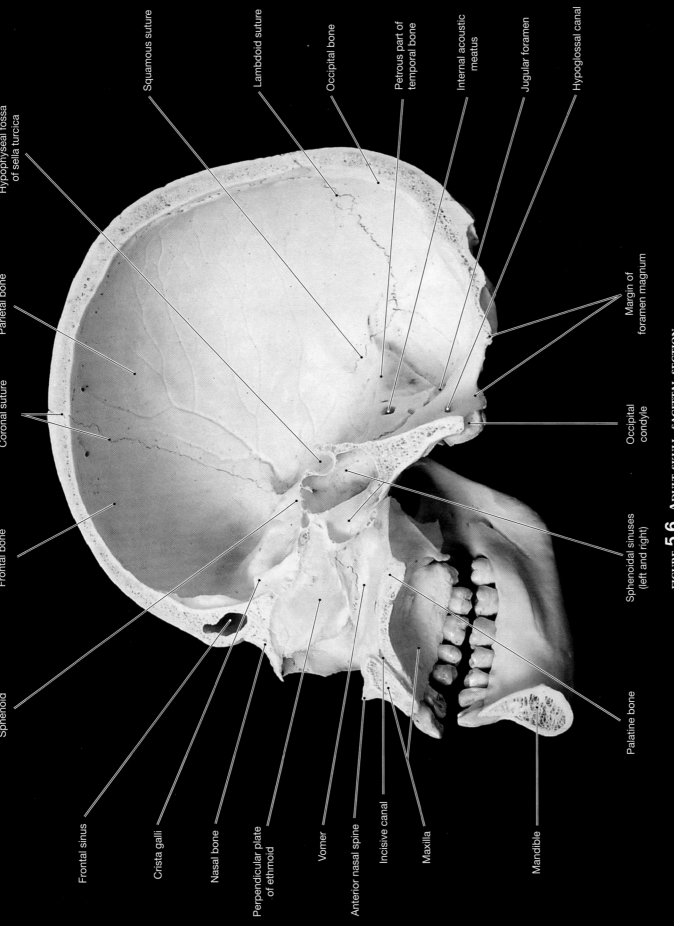

Hypophyseal fossa
of sella turcica

Squamous suture

Lambdoid suture

Occipital bone

Petrous part of
temporal bone

Internal acoustic
meatus

Jugular foramen

Hypoglossal canal

Parietal bone

Frontal bone

Coronal suture

Sphenoid

Frontal sinus

Crista galli

Nasal bone

Perpendicular plate
of ethmoid

Vomer

Anterior nasal spine

Incisive canal

Maxilla

Mandible

Palatine bone

Sphenoidal sinuses
(left and right)

Occipital
condyle

Margin of
foramen magnum

FIGURE 5.6 ADULT SKULL, SAGITTAL SECTION

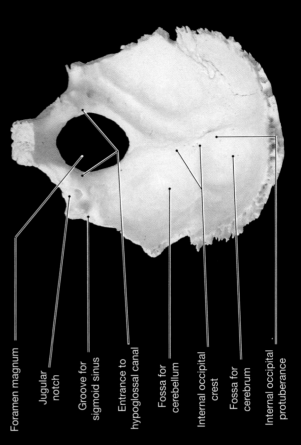

Foramen magnum

Jugular
notch

Groove for
sigmoid sinus

Entrance to
hypoglossal canal

Fossa for
cerebellum

Internal occipital
crest

Fossa for
cerebrum

Internal occipital
protuberance

FIGURE 6.1b OCCIPITAL BONE, SUPERIOR (INTERNAL) VIEW

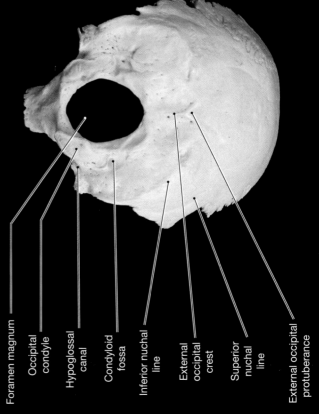

Foramen magnum

Occipital
condyle

Hypoglossal
canal

Condyloid
fossa

Inferior nuchal
line

External
occipital
crest

Superior
nuchal
line

External occipital
protuberance

FIGURE 6.1a OCCIPITAL BONE, INFERIOR (EXTERNAL) VIEW

Border of
sagittal suture

Parietal
eminence

Superior
temporal
line

Inferior
temporal
line

Border of
squamous suture

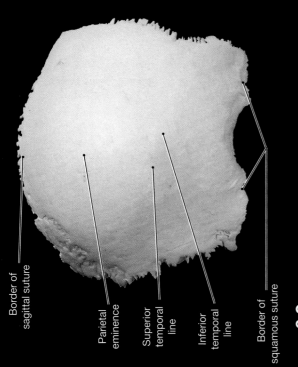

FIGURE **6.2** PARIETAL BONE, LATERAL VIEW

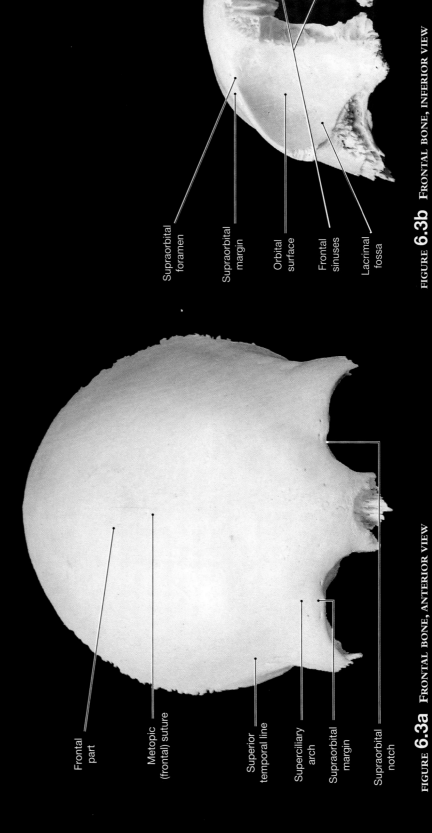

Supraorbital
foramen

Supraorbital
margin

Orbital
surface

Frontal
sinuses

Lacrimal
fossa

FIGURE **6.3b** FRONTAL BONE, INFERIOR VIEW

Frontal
part

Metopic
(frontal) suture

Superior
temporal line

Superciliary
arch

Supraorbital
margin

Supraorbital
notch

FIGURE **6.3a** FRONTAL BONE, ANTERIOR VIEW

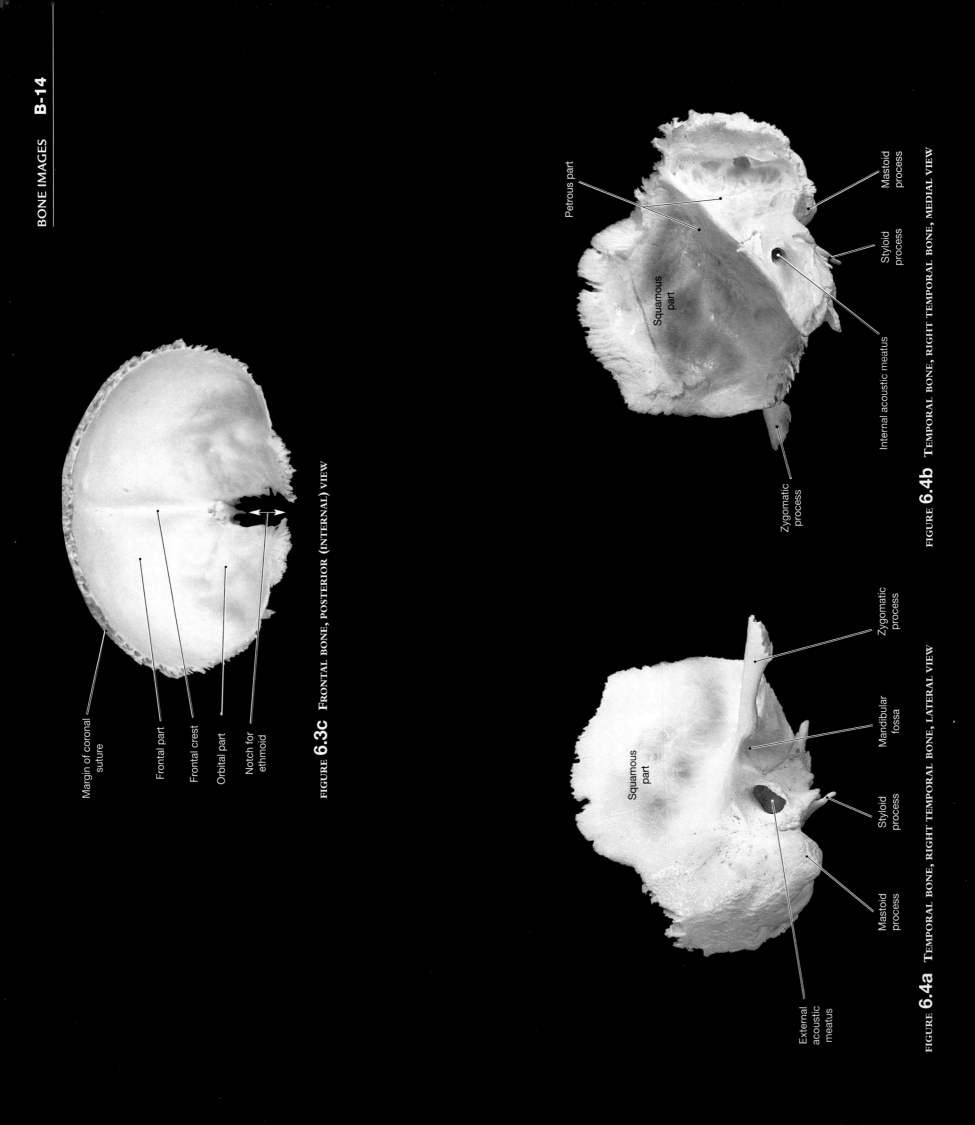

Margin of coronal suture

Frontal part

Frontal crest

Orbital part

Notch for ethmoid

FIGURE **6.3c** FRONTAL BONE, POSTERIOR (INTERNAL) VIEW

Petrous part

Squamous part

Mastoid process

Styloid process

Internal acoustic meatus

Zygomatic process

FIGURE **6.4b** TEMPORAL BONE, RIGHT TEMPORAL BONE, MEDIAL VIEW

Squamous part

Zygomatic process

Mandibular fossa

Styloid process

Mastoid process

External acoustic meatus

FIGURE **6.4a** TEMPORAL BONE, RIGHT TEMPORAL BONE, LATERAL VIEW

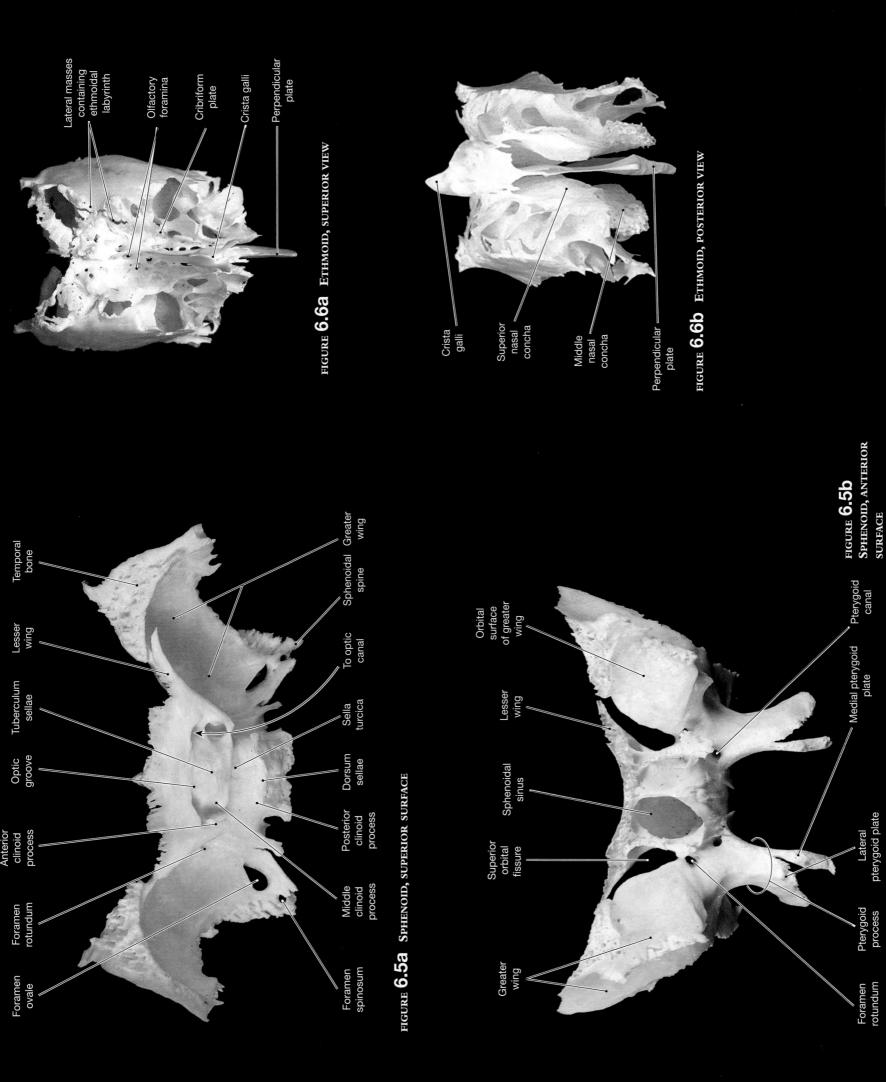

Lateral masses
containing
ethmoidal
labyrinth

Olfactory
foramina

Cribriform
plate

Crista galli

Perpendicular
plate

FIGURE 6.6a ETHMOID, SUPERIOR VIEW

Crista
galli

Superior
nasal
concha

Middle
nasal
concha

Perpendicular
plate

FIGURE 6.6b ETHMOID, POSTERIOR VIEW

Temporal
bone

Lesser
wing

Tuberculum
sellae

Optic
groove

Anterior
clinoid
process

Foramen
rotundum

Foramen
spinosum

Middle
clinoid
process

Posterior
clinoid
process

Dorsum
sellae

Sella
turcica

To optic
canal

Sphenoidal
spine

Greater
wing

FIGURE 6.5a SPHENOID, SUPERIOR SURFACE

Orbital
surface
of greater
wing

Lesser
wing

Sphenoidal
sinus

Superior
orbital
fissure

Greater
wing

Foramen
rotundum

Pterygoid
process

Lateral
pterygoid plate

Medial pterygoid
plate

Pterygoid
canal

FIGURE 6.5b
SPHENOID, ANTERIOR
SURFACE

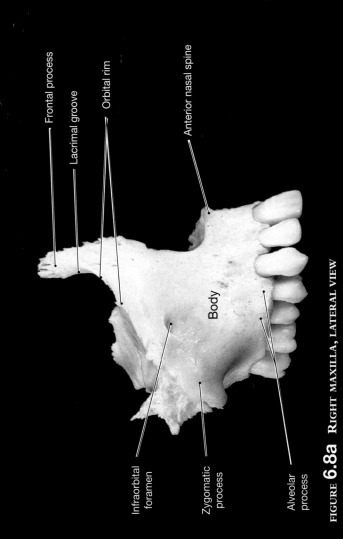

Frontal process

Lacrimal groove

Orbital rim

Anterior nasal spine

Body

Infraorbital foramen

Zygomatic process

Alveolar process

FIGURE 6.8a RIGHT MAXILLA, LATERAL VIEW

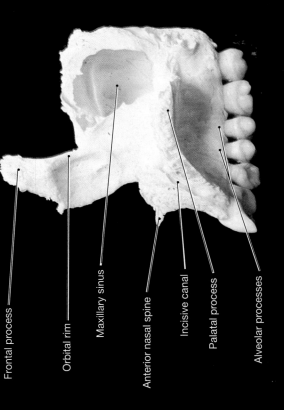

Frontal process

Orbital rim

Maxillary sinus

Anterior nasal spine

Incisive canal

Palatal process

Alveolar processes

FIGURE 6.8b RIGHT MAXILLA, MEDIAL VIEW

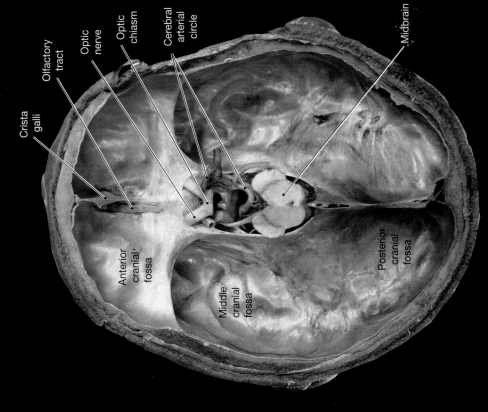

Crista galli

Olfactory tract

Optic nerve

Optic chiasm

Cerebral arterial circle

Midbrain

Anterior cranial fossa

Middle cranial fossa

Posterior cranial fossa

FIGURE 6.7 CRANIAL FOSSAE, SUPERIOR VIEW

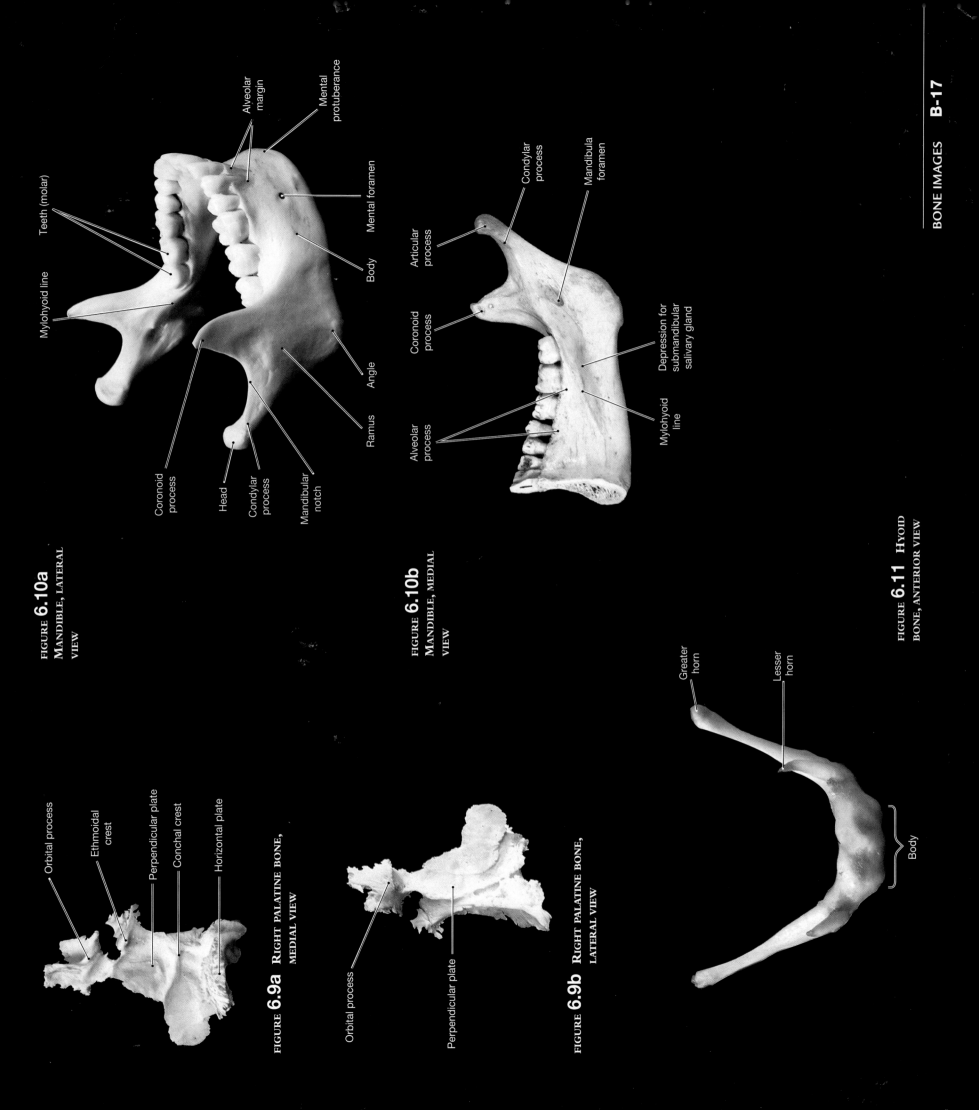

Teeth (molar)

Alveolar margin

Mental protuberance

Mental foramen

Body

Mylohyoid line

Angle

Ramus

Coronoid process

Head

Condylar process

Mandibular notch

FIGURE 6.10a MANDIBLE, LATERAL VIEW

Articular process

Condylar process

Mandibula foramen

Coronoid process

Depression for submandibular salivary gland

Alveolar process

Mylohyoid line

FIGURE 6.10b MANDIBLE, MEDIAL VIEW

FIGURE 6.11 HYOID BONE, ANTERIOR VIEW

Greater horn

Lesser horn

Body

Orbital process

Ethmoidal crest

Perpendicular plate

Conchal crest

Horizontal plate

FIGURE 6.9a RIGHT PALATINE BONE, MEDIAL VIEW

Orbital process

Perpendicular plate

FIGURE 6.9b RIGHT PALATINE BONE, LATERAL VIEW

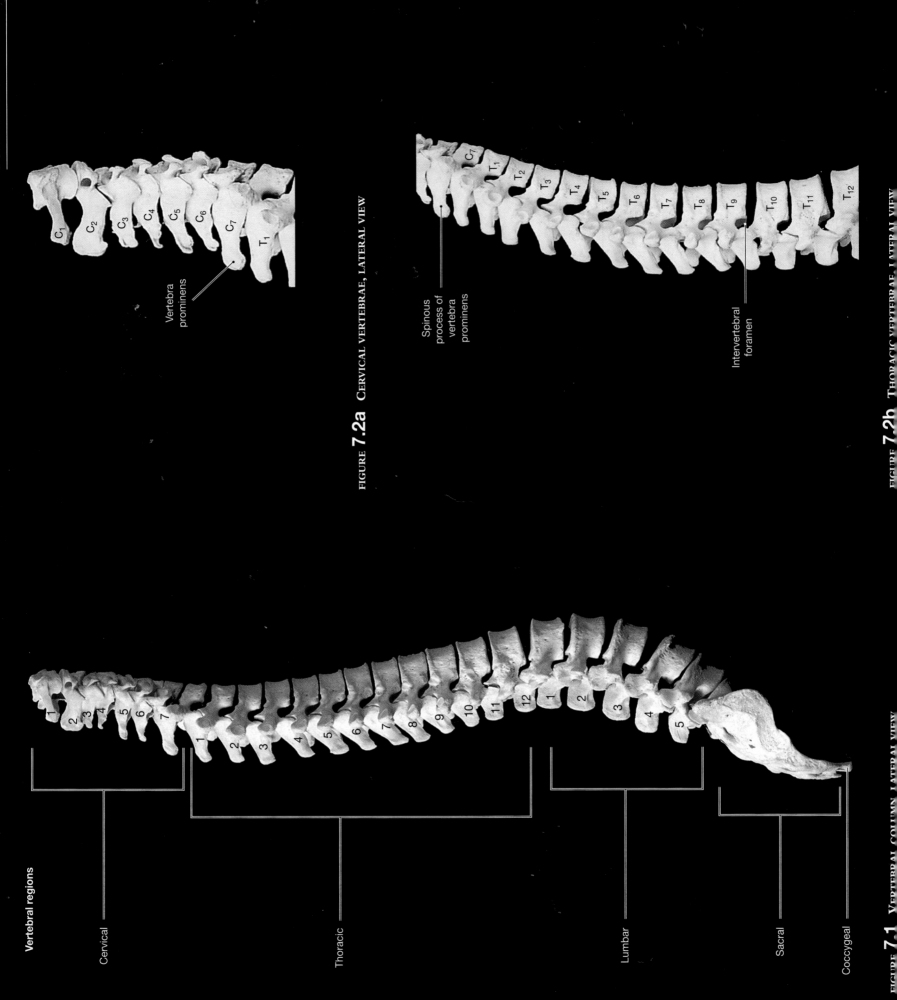

FIGURE **7.2a** CERVICAL VERTEBRAE, LATERAL VIEW

Vertebra prominens

Spinous process of vertebra prominens

Intervertebral foramen

FIGURE **7.2b** THORACIC VERTEBRAE, LATERAL VIEW

Vertebral regions

Cervical

Thoracic

Lumbar

Sacral

Coccygeal

FIGURE **7.1** VERTEBRAL COLUMN, LATERAL VIEW

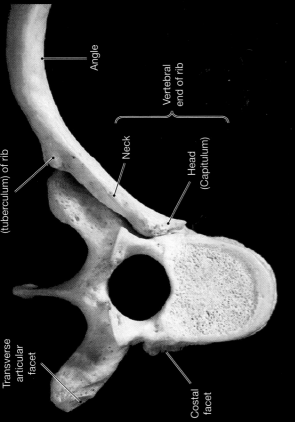

Transverse
articular
facet

(tuberculum) of rib

Angle

Neck

Vertebral
end of rib

Head
(Capitulum)

Costal
facet

FIGURE 7.3a THORACIC VERTEBRA AND RIB, SUPERIOR VIEW

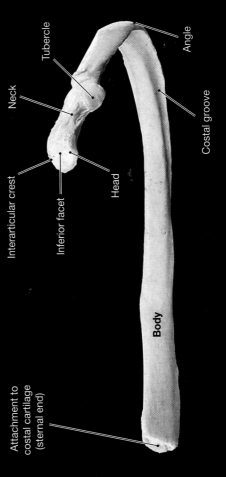

Tubercle

Neck

Angle

Interarticular crest

Inferior facet

Head

Costal groove

Attachment to
costal cartilage
(sternal end)

Body

FIGURE 7.3b RIB, POSTERIOR AND MEDIAL VIEW

L1
L2
L3
L4
L5

Sacrum

FIGURE 7.2c LUMBAR VERTEBRAE, LATERAL VIEW

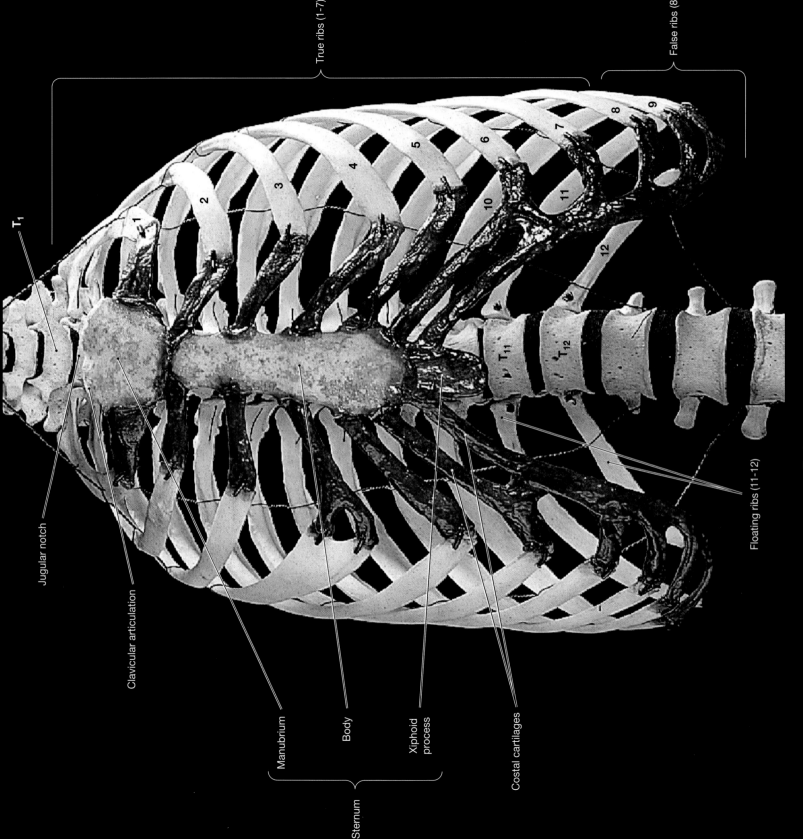

True ribs (1-7)

False ribs (8-

T₁

1
2
3
4
5
6
7
8
9
10
11
12

T₁₁
T₁₂

Jugular notch

Clavicular articulation

Manubrium

Body

Xiphoid process

Costal cartilages

Sternum

Floating ribs (11-12)

FIGURE **7.4** THORACIC CAGE, ANTERIOR VIEW

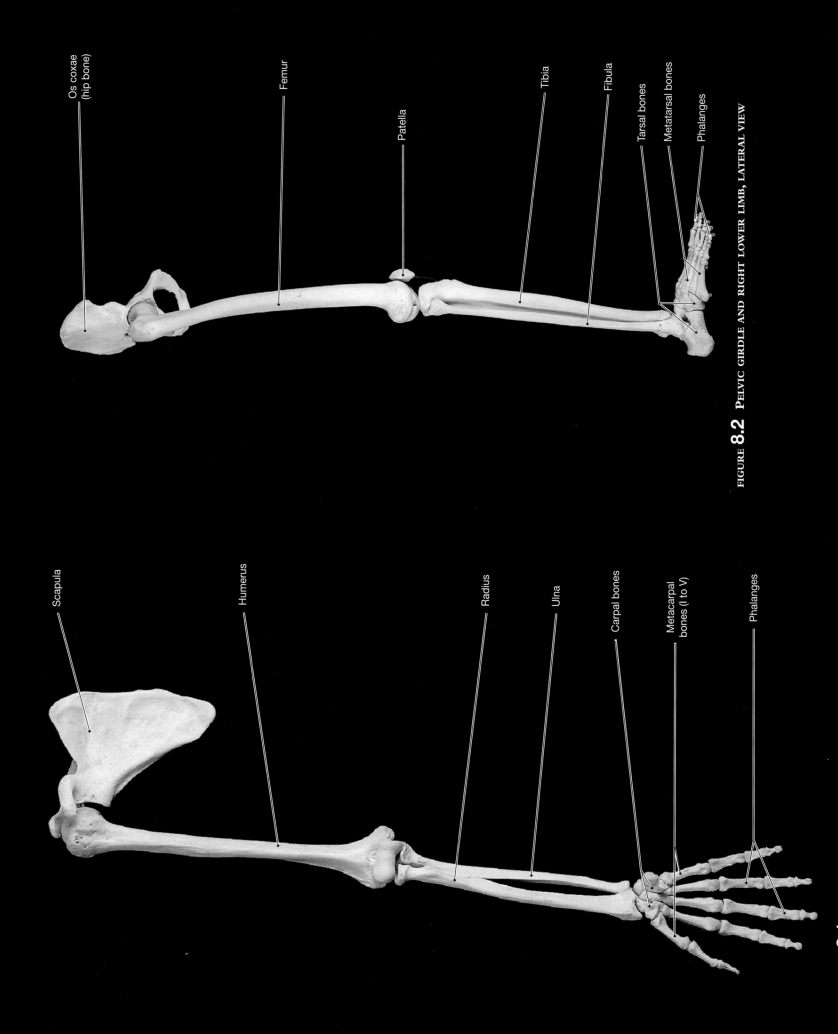

Os coxae
(hip bone)

Femur

Patella

Tibia

Fibula

Tarsal bones

Metatarsal bones

Phalanges

FIGURE **8.2** PELVIC GIRDLE AND RIGHT LOWER LIMB, LATERAL VIEW

Scapula

Humerus

Radius

Ulna

Carpal bones

Metacarpal
bones (I to V)

Phalanges

FIGURE **8.1** PECTORAL GIRDLE AND RIGHT UPPER LIMB, ANTERIOR VIEW

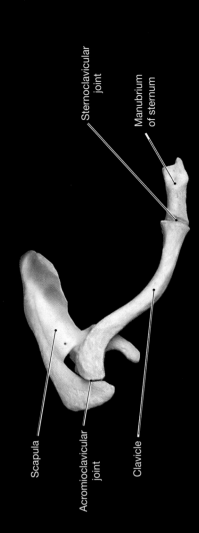

Scapula

Acromioclavicular
joint

Clavicle

Sternoclavicular
joint

Manubrium
of sternum

FIGURE **8.4** RIGHT PECTORAL GIRDLE, SUPERIOR VIEW

Sternal
end

Facet for articulation
with sternum

Acromial
end

Facet for articulation
with acromion

FIGURE **8.3a** RIGHT CLAVICLE, SUPERIOR VIEW

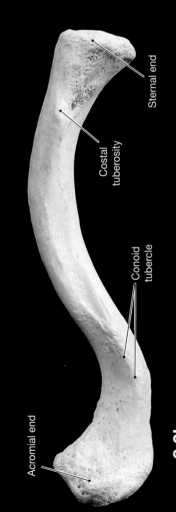

Sternal end

Costal
tuberosity

Conoid
tubercle

Acromial end

FIGURE **8.3b** RIGHT CLAVICLE, INFERIOR VIEW

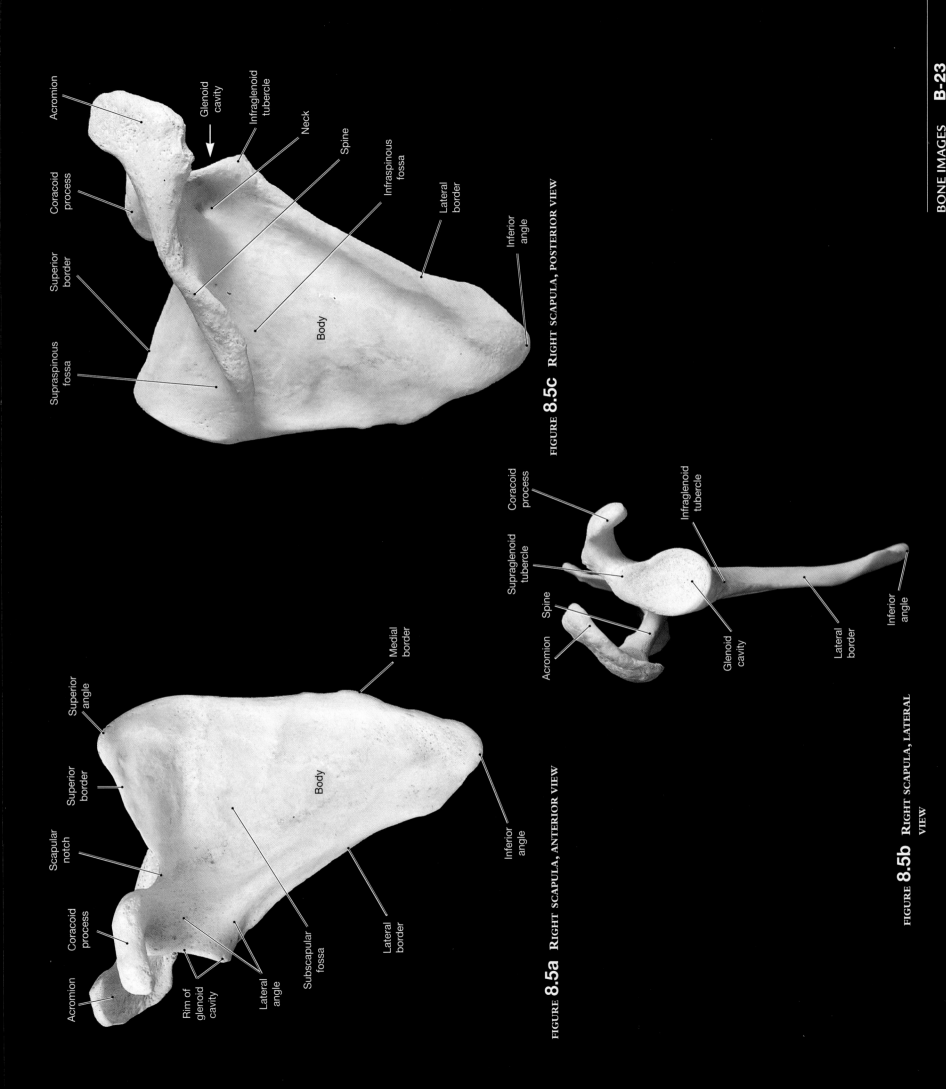

Acromion

Glenoid
cavity

Infraglenoid
tubercle

Neck

Spine

Coracoid
process

Infraspinous
fossa

Superior
border

Lateral
border

Supraspinous
fossa

Body

Inferior
angle

FIGURE 8.5c RIGHT SCAPULA, POSTERIOR VIEW

Coracoid
process

Supraglenoid
tubercle

Infraglenoid
tubercle

Spine

Acromion

Glenoid
cavity

Lateral
border

Inferior
angle

FIGURE 8.5b RIGHT SCAPULA, LATERAL
VIEW

Superior
angle

Scapular
notch

Superior
border

Medial
border

Coracoid
process

Body

Acromion

Rim of
glenoid
cavity

Lateral
angle

Subscapular
fossa

Lateral
border

Inferior
angle

FIGURE 8.5a RIGHT SCAPULA, ANTERIOR VIEW

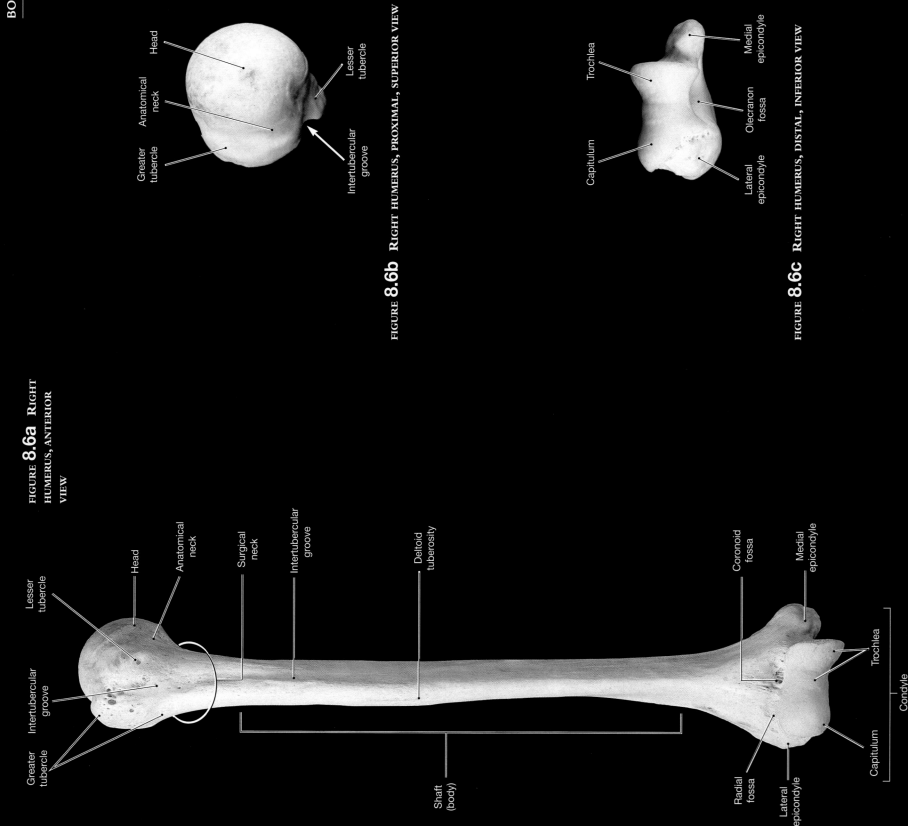

FIGURE **8.6a** **RIGHT HUMERUS, ANTERIOR VIEW**

Lesser tubercle

Head

Anatomical neck

Surgical neck

Intertubercular groove

Deltoid tuberosity

Coronoid fossa

Medial epicondyle

Greater tubercle

Intertubercular groove

Shaft (body)

Trochlea

Condyle

Radial fossa

Lateral epicondyle

Capitulum

FIGURE **8.6b** **RIGHT HUMERUS, PROXIMAL, SUPERIOR VIEW**

Head

Anatomical neck

Greater tubercle

Lesser tubercle

Intertubercular groove

FIGURE **8.6c** **RIGHT HUMERUS, DISTAL, INFERIOR VIEW**

Trochlea

Capitulum

Medial epicondyle

Olecranon fossa

Lateral epicondyle

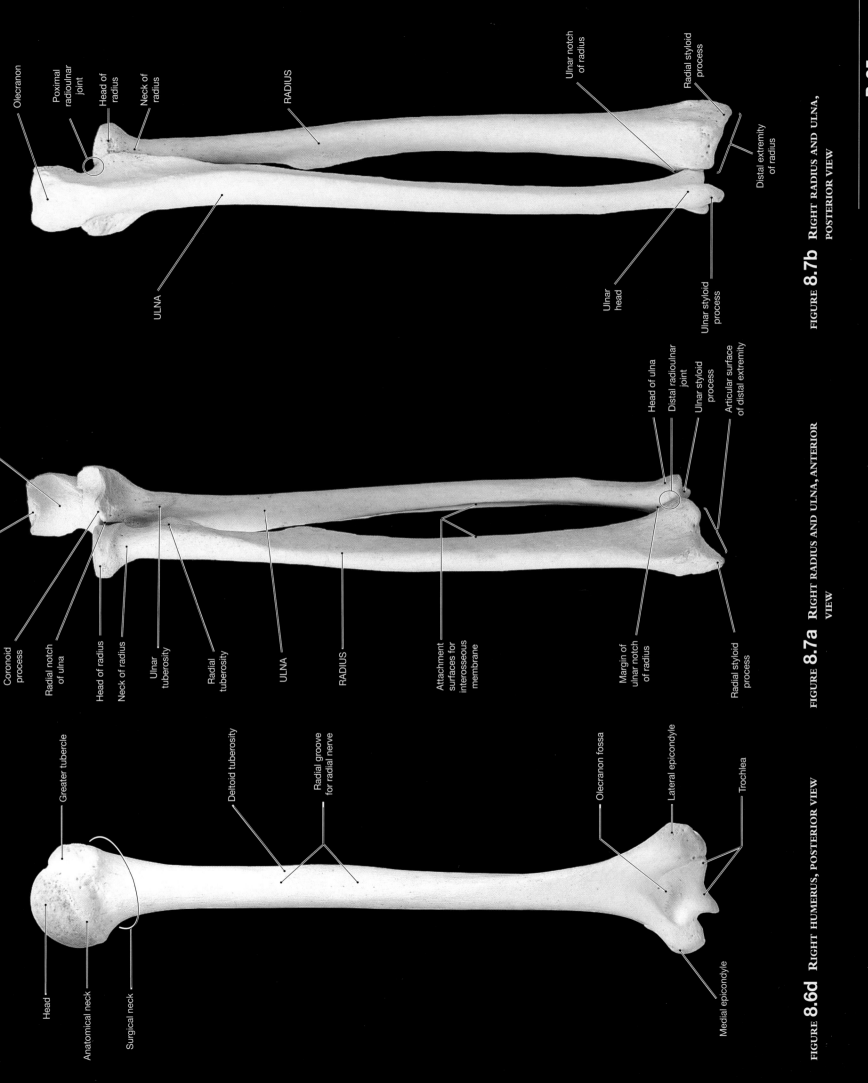

Olecranon

Poximal radioulnar joint

Head of radius

Neck of radius

RADIUS

ULNA

Ulnar notch of radius

Radial styloid process

Distal extremity of radius

Ulnar head

Ulnar styloid process

FIGURE **8.7b** **RIGHT RADIUS AND ULNA, POSTERIOR VIEW**

Coronoid process

Radial notch of ulna

Head of radius

Neck of radius

Ulnar tuberosity

Radial tuberosity

ULNA

RADIUS

Attachment surfaces for interosseous membrane

Margin of ulnar notch of radius

Radial styloid process

Head of ulna

Distal radioulnar joint

Ulnar styloid process

Articular surface of distal extremity

FIGURE **8.7a** **RIGHT RADIUS AND ULNA, ANTERIOR VIEW**

Greater tubercle

Head

Anatomical neck

Surgical neck

Deltoid tuberosity

Radial groove for radial nerve

Olecranon fossa

Lateral epicondyle

Trochlea

Medial epicondyle

FIGURE **8.6d** **RIGHT HUMERUS, POSTERIOR VIEW**

BONE IMAGES   **B-25**

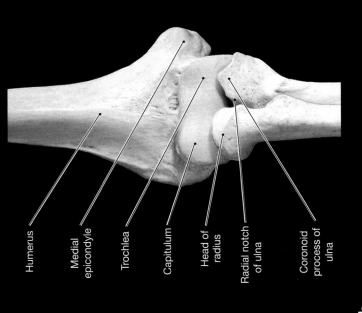

Humerus

Medial
epicondyle

Trochlea

Capitulum

Head of
radius

Radial notch
of ulna

Coronoid
process of
ulna

FIGURE 8.8b RIGHT ELBOW JOINT, ANTERIOR VIEW

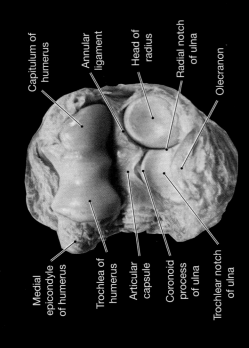

Capitulum of
humerus

Annular
ligament

Head of
radius

Radial notch
of ulna

Olecranon

Medial
epicondyle
of humerus

Trochlea of
humerus

Articular
capsule

Coronoid
process
of ulna

Trochlear notch
of ulna

FIGURE 8.8d RIGHT ELBOW JOINT, ARTICULAR SURFACES

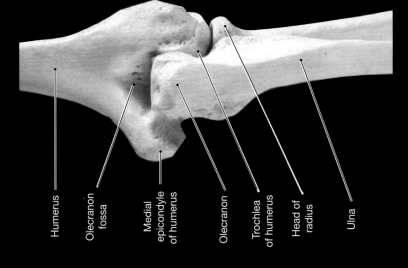

Humerus

Olecranon
fossa

Medial
epicondyle
of humerus

Olecranon

Trochlea
of humerus

Head of
radius

Ulna

FIGURE 8.8a RIGHT ELBOW JOINT, POSTERIOR VIEW

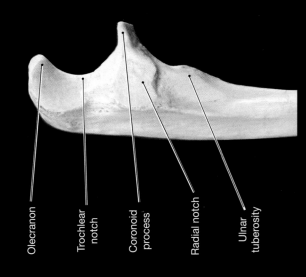

Olecranon

Trochlear
notch

Coronoid
process

Radial notch

Ulnar
tuberosity

FIGURE 8.8c RIGHT ULNA, PROXIMAL, LATERAL VIEW

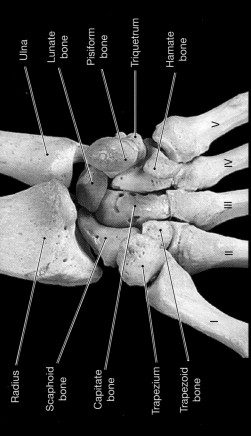

Ulna
Lunate bone
Pisiform bone
Triquetrum
Hamate bone

Radius
Scaphoid bone
Capitate bone
Trapezium
Trapezoid bone

FIGURE **8.9**   **R**IGHT WRIST, ANTERIOR (PALMAR) VIEW

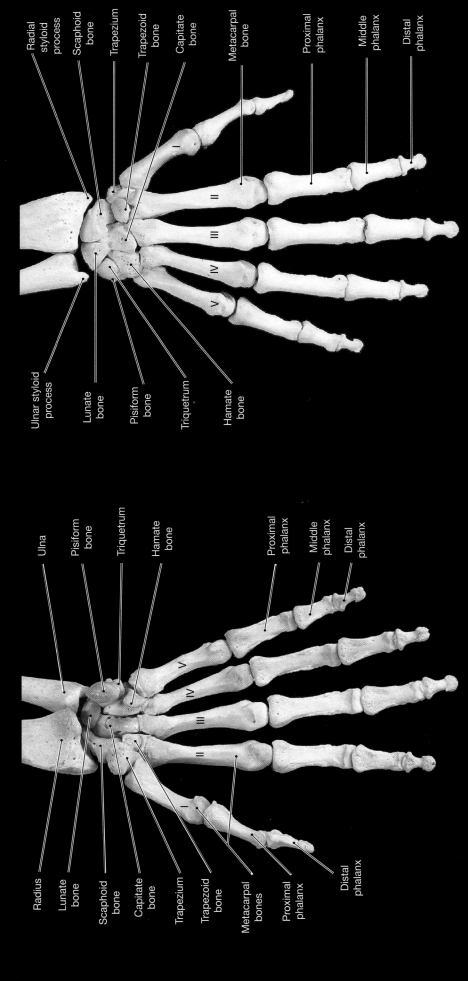

Radial styloid process
Scaphoid bone
Trapezium
Trapezoid bone
Capitate bone
Metacarpal bone
Proximal phalanx
Middle phalanx
Distal phalanx

Ulnar styloid process
Lunate bone
Pisiform bone
Triquetrum
Hamate bone

FIGURE **8.10b**   **R**IGHT HAND, POSTERIOR (DORSAL) VIEW

Ulna
Pisiform bone
Triquetrum
Hamate bone
Proximal phalanx
Middle phalanx
Distal phalanx

Radius
Lunate bone
Scaphoid bone
Capitate bone
Trapezium
Trapezoid bone
Metacarpal bones
Proximal phalanx
Distal phalanx

FIGURE **8.10a**   **R**IGHT HAND, ANTERIOR (PALMAR) VIEW

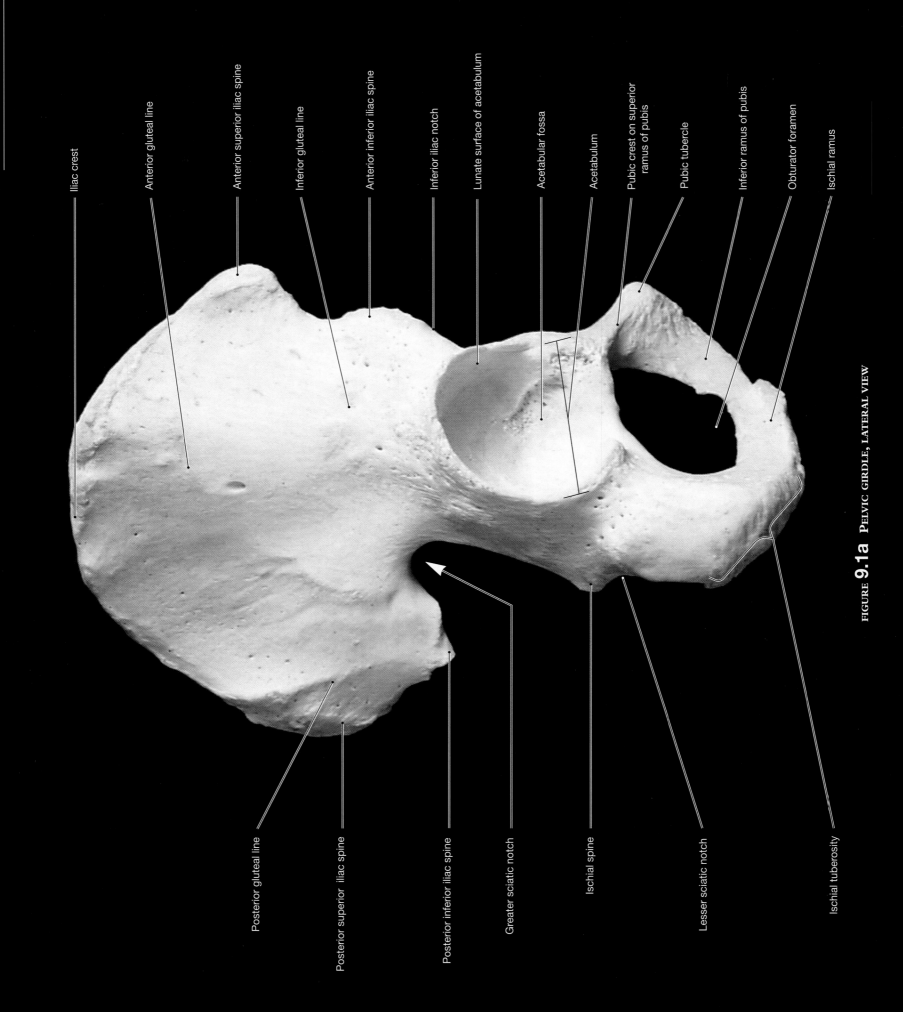

Iliac crest

Anterior gluteal line

Anterior superior iliac spine

Inferior gluteal line

Anterior inferior iliac spine

Inferior iliac notch

Lunate surface of acetabulum

Acetabular fossa

Acetabulum

Pubic crest on superior ramus of pubis

Pubic tubercle

Inferior ramus of pubis

Obturator foramen

Ischial ramus

Posterior gluteal line

Posterior superior iliac spine

Posterior inferior iliac spine

Greater sciatic notch

Ischial spine

Lesser sciatic notch

Ischial tuberosity

FIGURE **9.1a** PELVIC GIRDLE, LATERAL VIEW

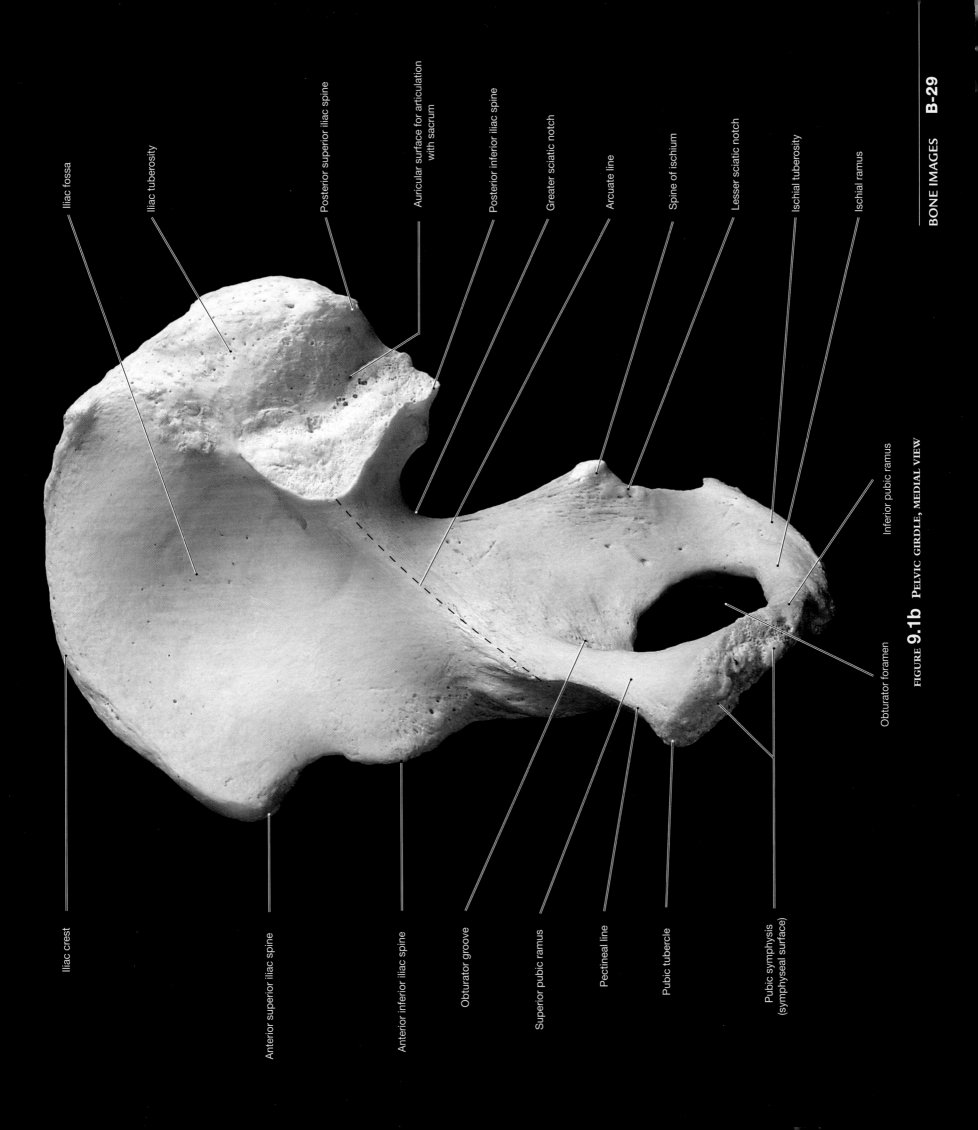

Iliac fossa

Iliac tuberosity

Posterior superior iliac spine

Auricular surface for articulation with sacrum

Posterior inferior iliac spine

Greater sciatic notch

Arcuate line

Spine of ischium

Lesser sciatic notch

Ischial tuberosity

Ischial ramus

Iliac crest

Anterior superior iliac spine

Anterior inferior iliac spine

Obturator groove

Superior pubic ramus

Pectineal line

Pubic tubercle

Pubic symphysis (symphyseal surface)

Obturator foramen

Inferior pubic ramus

FIGURE **9.1b** PELVIC GIRDLE, MEDIAL VIEW

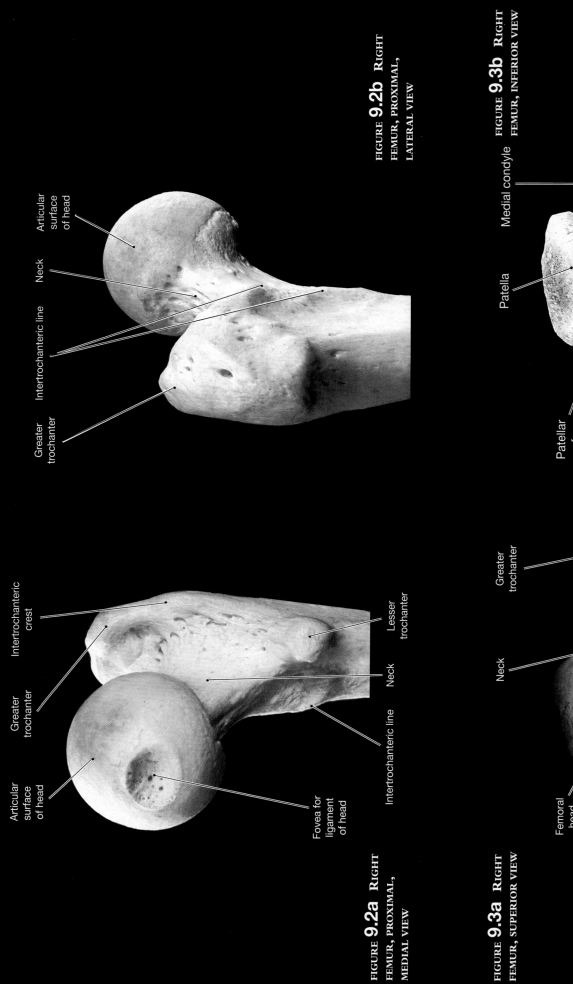

Articular
surface
of head

Intertrochanteric
crest

Greater
trochanter

Neck

Intertrochanteric line

Fovea for
ligament
of head

Lesser
trochanter

FIGURE **9.2a** RIGHT
FEMUR, PROXIMAL,
MEDIAL VIEW

Articular
surface
of head

Neck

Intertrochanteric line

Greater
trochanter

FIGURE **9.2b** RIGHT
FEMUR, PROXIMAL,
LATERAL VIEW

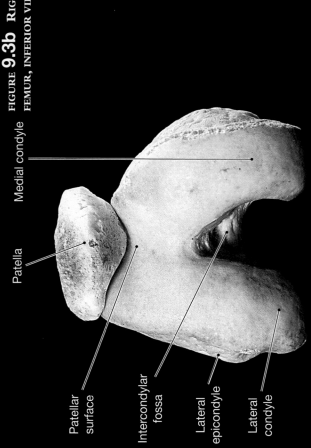

Medial condyle

Patella

Patellar
surface

Intercondylar
fossa

Lateral
epicondyle

Lateral
condyle

FIGURE **9.3b** RIGHT
FEMUR, INFERIOR VIEW

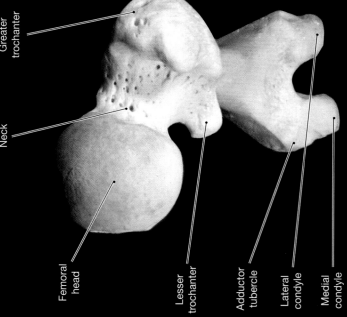

Greater
trochanter

Neck

Femoral
head

Lesser
trochanter

Adductor
tubercle

Lateral
condyle

Medial
condyle

FIGURE **9.3a** RIGHT
FEMUR, SUPERIOR VIEW

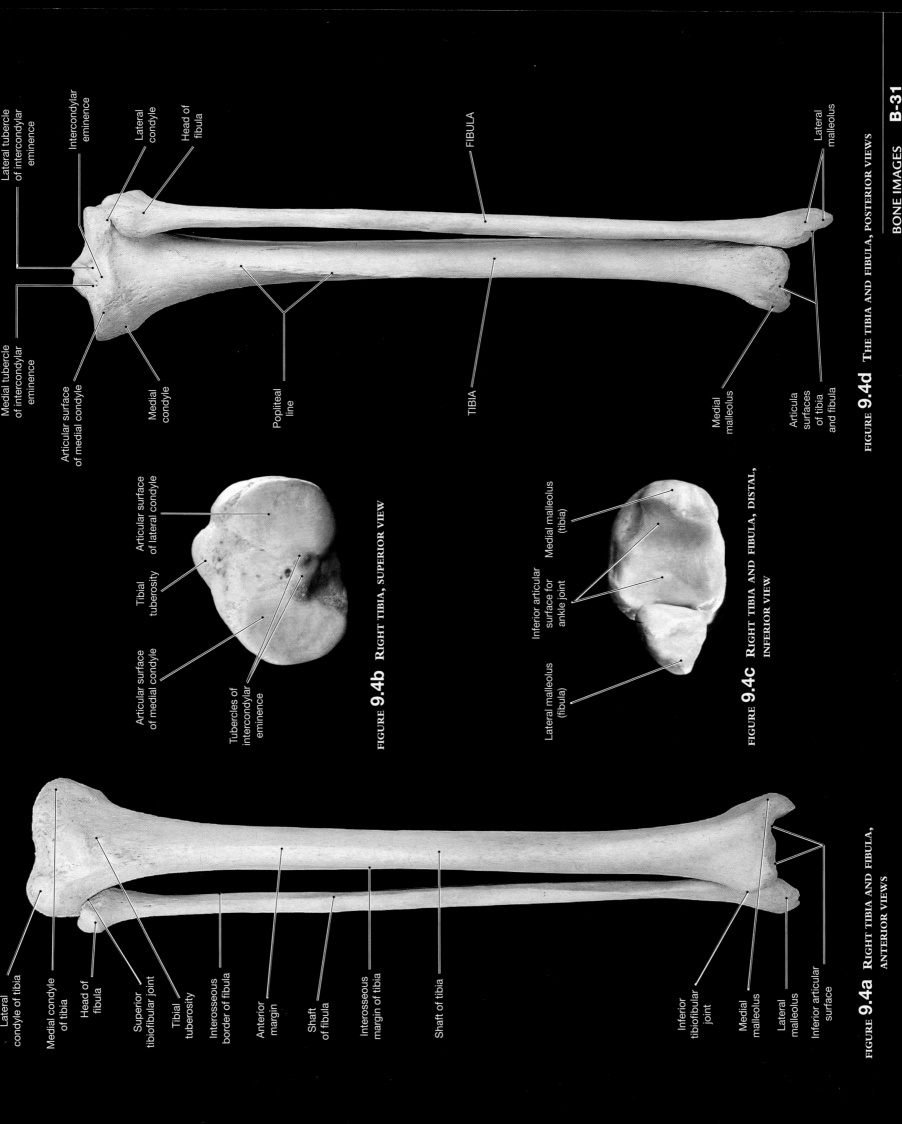

Lateral tubercle of intercondylar eminence

Intercondylar eminence

Lateral condyle

Head of fibula

FIBULA

Lateral malleolus

Medial tubercle of intercondylar eminence

Articular surface of medial condyle

Medial condyle

Popliteal line

TIBIA

Medial malleolus

Articula surfaces of tibia and fibula

FIGURE 9.4d THE TIBIA AND FIBULA, POSTERIOR VIEWS

Tibial tuberosity

Articular surface of lateral condyle

Articular surface of medial condyle

Tubercles of intercondylar eminence

FIGURE 9.4b RIGHT TIBIA, SUPERIOR VIEW

Medial malleolus (tibia)

Inferior articular surface for ankle joint

Lateral malleolus (fibula)

FIGURE 9.4c RIGHT TIBIA AND FIBULA, DISTAL, INFERIOR VIEW

Lateral condyle of tibia

Medial condyle of tibia

Head of fibula

Superior tibiofibular joint

Tibial tuberosity

Interosseous border of fibula

Anterior margin

Shaft of fibula

Interosseous margin of tibia

Shaft of tibia

Inferior tibiofibular joint

Medial malleolus

Lateral malleolus

Inferior articular surface

FIGURE 9.4a RIGHT TIBIA AND FIBULA, ANTERIOR VIEWS

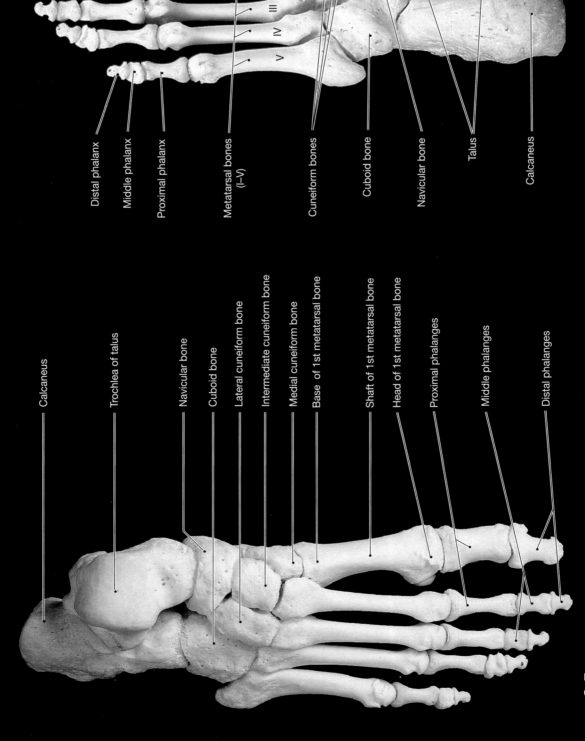

Distal phalanx

Proximal phalanx

I
II
III
IV
V

Distal phalanx

Middle phalanx

Proximal phalanx

Metatarsal bones
(I–V)

Cuneiform bones

Cuboid bone

Navicular bone

Talus

Calcaneus

FIGURE **9.5b** RIGHT FOOT, INFERIOR (PLANTAR) VIEW

Calcaneus

Trochlea of talus

Navicular bone

Cuboid bone

Lateral cuneiform bone

Intermediate cuneiform bone

Medial cuneiform bone

Base of 1st metatarsal bone

Shaft of 1st metatarsal bone

Head of 1st metatarsal bone

Proximal phalanges

Middle phalanges

Distal phalanges

FIGURE **9.5a** RIGHT FOOT, SUPERIOR (DORSAL) VIEW

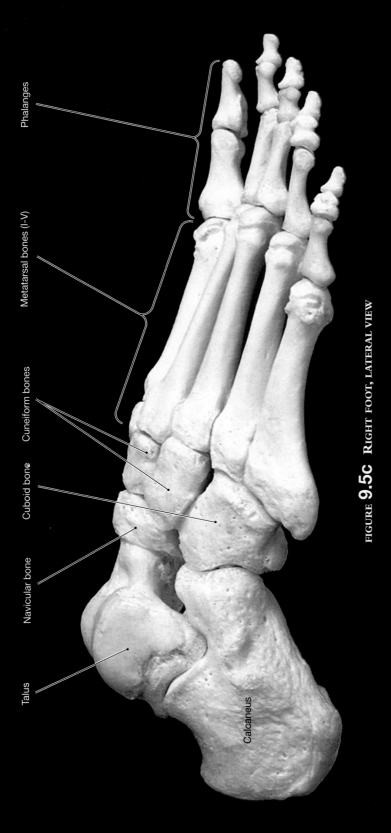

Phalanges

Metatarsal bones (I–V)

Cuneiform bones

Cuboid bone

Navicular bone

Talus

Calcaneus

FIGURE **9.5c** RIGHT FOOT, LATERAL VIEW

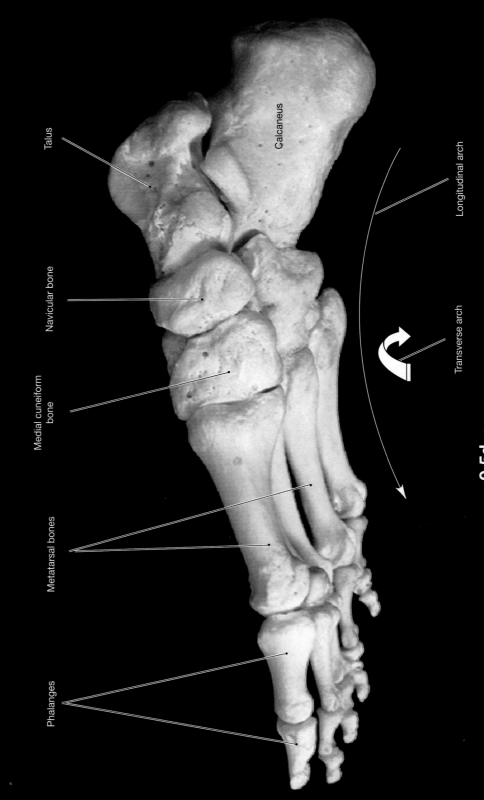

Talus

Navicular bone

Medial cuneiform bone

Metatarsal bones

Phalanges

Calcaneus

Longitudinal arch

Transverse arch

FIGURE **9.5d** RIGHT FOOT, MEDIAL VIEW

CADAVER IMAGES

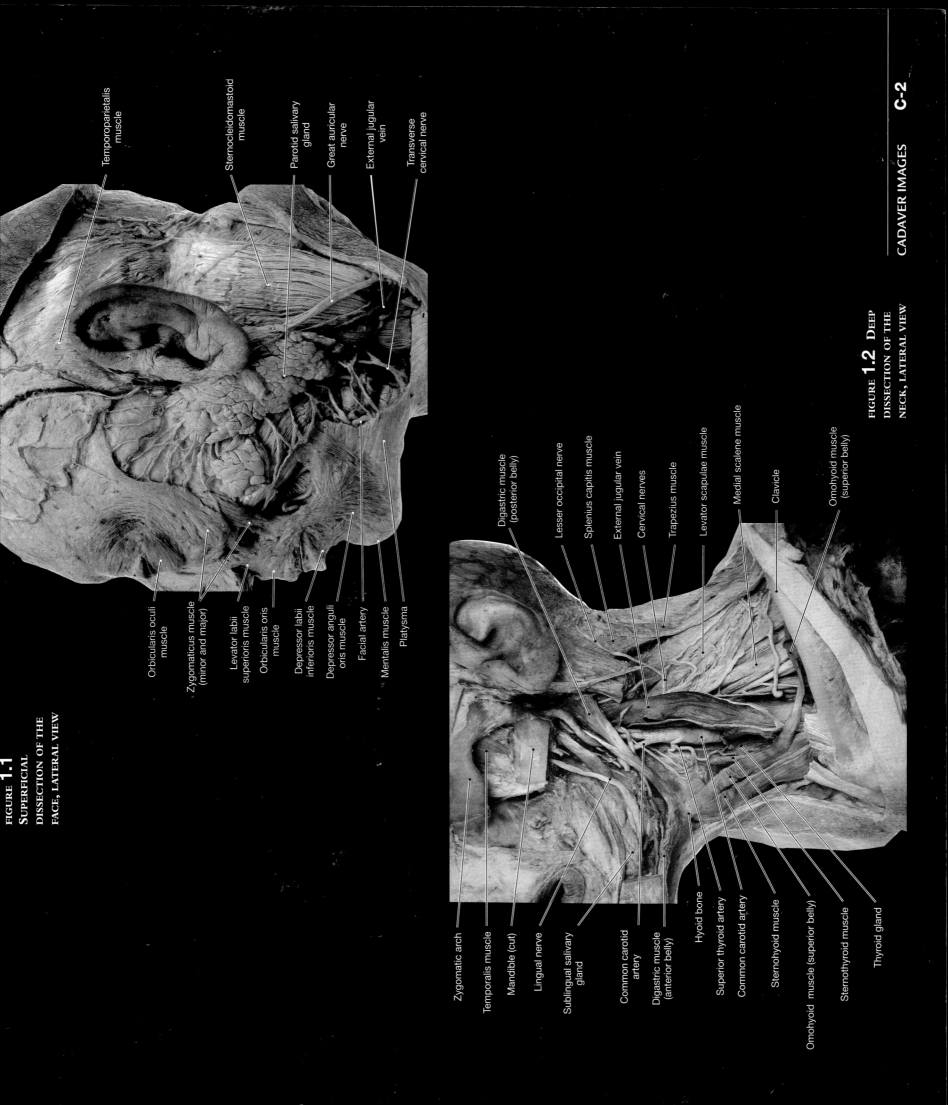

FIGURE 1.1
SUPERFICIAL DISSECTION OF THE FACE, LATERAL VIEW

Temporoparietalis muscle

Sternocleidomastoid muscle

Parotid salivary gland

Great auricular nerve

External jugular vein

Transverse cervical nerve

Orbicularis oculi muscle

Zygomaticus muscle (minor and major)

Levator labii superioris muscle

Orbicularis oris muscle

Depressor labii inferioris muscle

Depressor anguli oris muscle

Facial artery

Mentalis muscle

Platysma

FIGURE 1.2 DEEP DISSECTION OF THE NECK, LATERAL VIEW

Digastric muscle (posterior belly)

Lesser occipital nerve

Splenius capitis muscle

External jugular vein

Cervical nerves

Trapezius muscle

Levator scapulae muscle

Medial scalene muscle

Clavicle

Omohyoid muscle (superior belly)

Zygomatic arch

Temporalis muscle

Mandible (cut)

Lingual nerve

Sublingual salivary gland

Common carotid artery

Digastric muscle (anterior belly)

Hyoid bone

Superior thyroid artery

Common carotid artery

Sternohyoid muscle

Omohyoid muscle (superior belly)

Sternothyroid muscle

Thyroid gland

FIGURE **1.3** SURFACE
ANATOMY OF THE
ANTERIOR NECK

FIGURE **1.5**
SHOULDER AND NECK,
ANTERIOR VIEW

FIGURE **1.4**
DISSECTION OF THE
ANTERIOR NECK

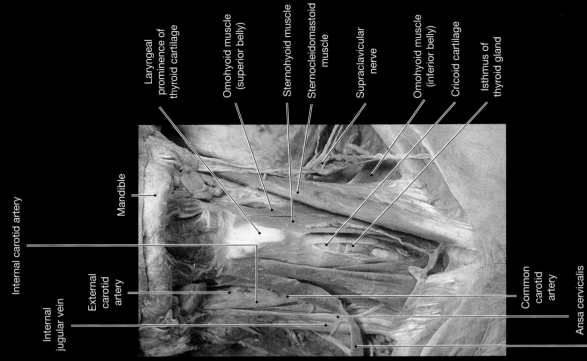

Internal carotid artery

Laryngeal
prominence of
thyroid cartilage

Omohyoid muscle
(superior belly)

Sternohyoid muscle

Sternocleidomastoid
muscle

Supraclavicular
nerve

Omohyoid muscle
(inferior belly)

Cricoid cartilage

Isthmus of
thyroid gland

Mandible

External
carotid
artery

Internal
jugular vein

Common
carotid
artery

Ansa cervicalis

Omohyoid muscle
(inferior belly)

Thyroid cartilage
of the larynx

Platysma

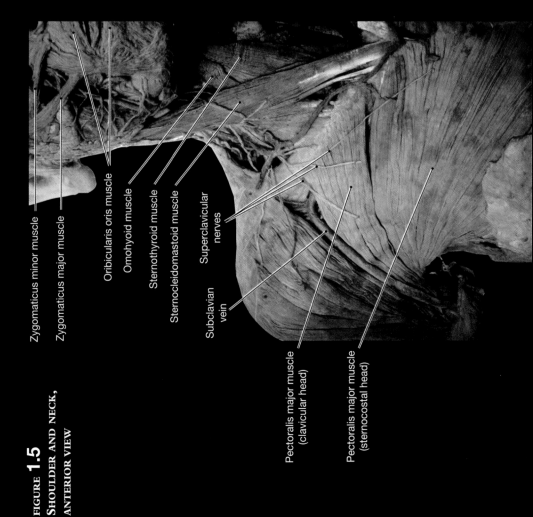

Zygomaticus minor muscle

Zygomaticus major muscle

Oribicularis oris muscle

Omohyoid muscle

Sternothyroid muscle

Sternocleidomastoid muscle

Superclavicular
nerves

Subclavian
vein

Pectoralis major muscle
(clavicular head)

Pectoralis major muscle
(sternocostal head)

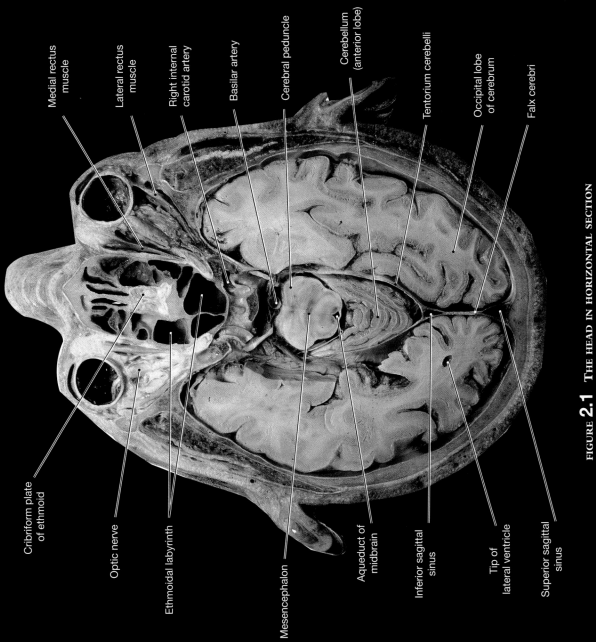

Medial rectus
muscle

Lateral rectus
muscle

Right internal
carotid artery

Basilar artery

Cerebral peduncle

Cerebellum
(anterior lobe)

Tentorium cerebelli

Occipital lobe
of cerebrum

Falx cerebri

Cribriform plate
of ethmoid

Optic nerve

Ethmoidal labyrinth

Mesencephalon

Aqueduct of
midbrain

Inferior sagittal
sinus

Tip of
lateral ventricle

Superior sagittal
sinus

FIGURE 2.1 THE HEAD IN HORIZONTAL SECTION

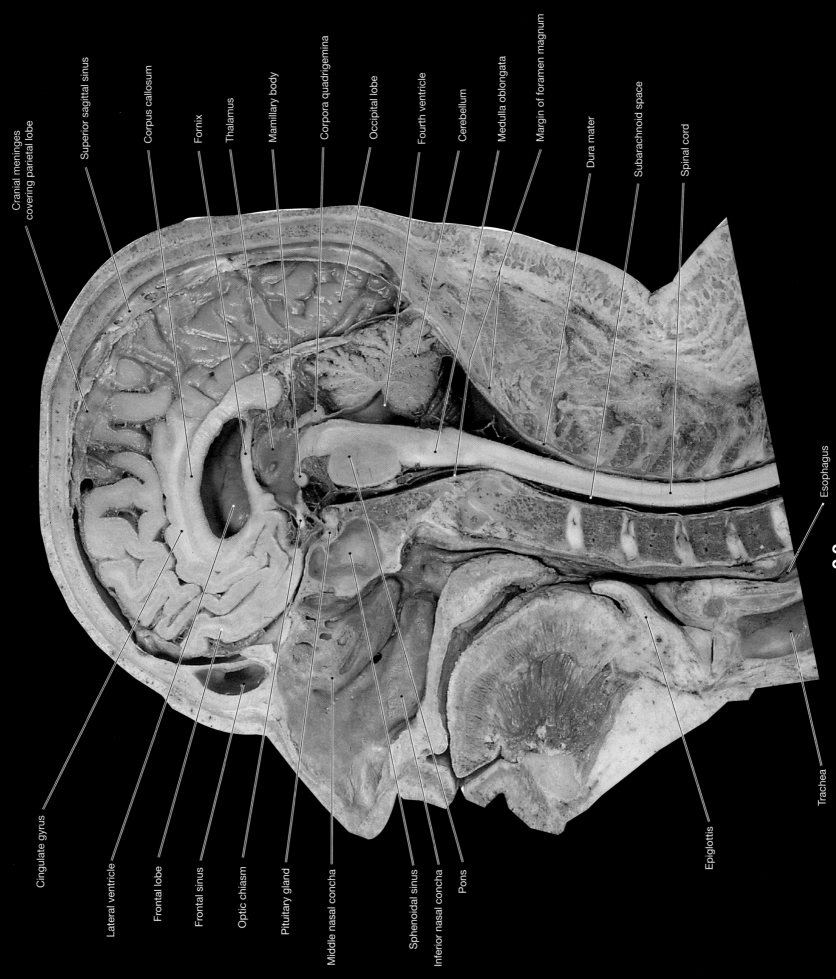

Cranial meninges covering parietal lobe

Superior sagittal sinus

Corpus callosum

Fornix

Thalamus

Mamillary body

Corpora quadrigemina

Occipital lobe

Fourth ventricle

Cerebellum

Medulla oblongata

Margin of foramen magnum

Dura mater

Subarachnoid space

Spinal cord

Cingulate gyrus

Lateral ventricle

Frontal lobe

Frontal sinus

Optic chiasm

Pituitary gland

Middle nasal concha

Sphenoidal sinus

Inferior nasal concha

Pons

Epiglottis

Esophagus

Trachea

FIGURE 2.2 THE HEAD IN SAGITTAL SECTION

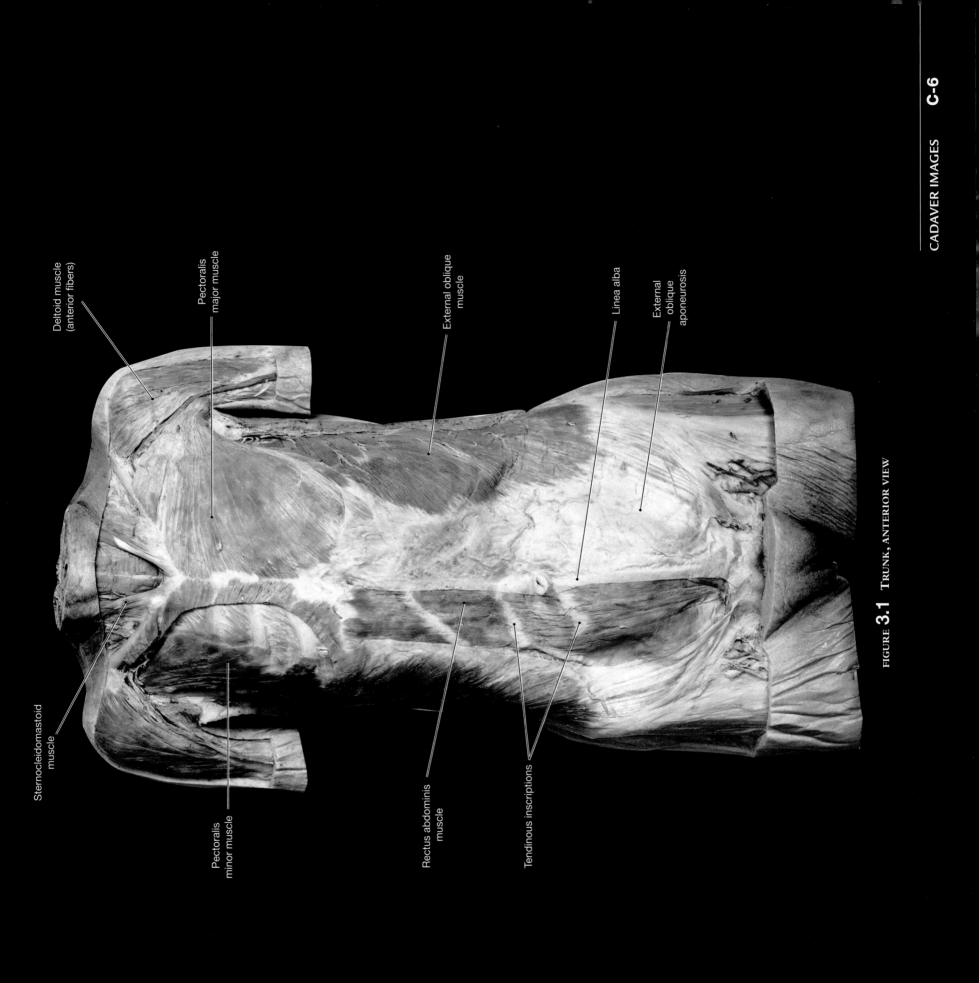

Deltoid muscle
(anterior fibers)

Pectoralis
major muscle

External oblique
muscle

Linea alba

External
oblique
aponeurosis

Sternocleidomastoid
muscle

Pectoralis
minor muscle

Rectus abdominis
muscle

Tendinous inscriptions

FIGURE **3.1** TRUNK, ANTERIOR VIEW

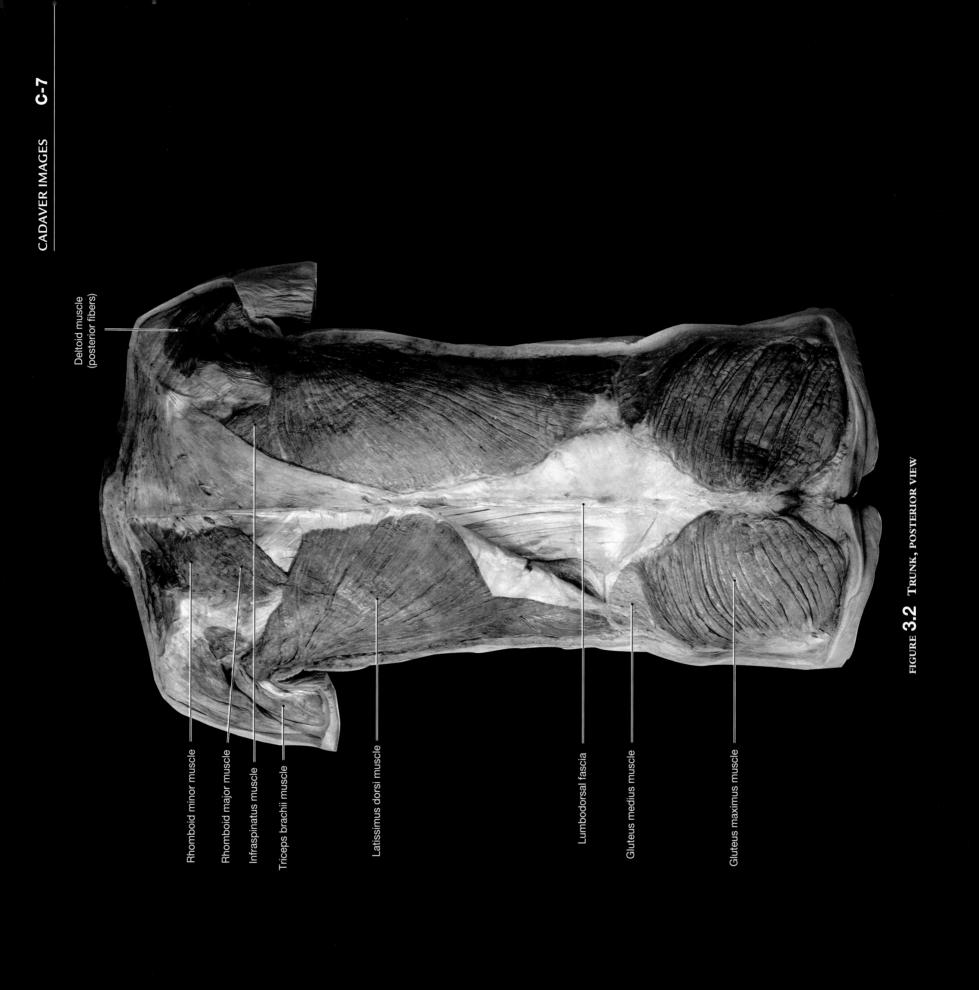

Deltoid muscle
(posterior fibers)

Rhomboid minor muscle

Rhomboid major muscle

Infraspinatus muscle

Triceps brachii muscle

Latissimus dorsi muscle

Lumbodorsal fascia

Gluteus medius muscle

Gluteus maximus muscle

FIGURE **3.2** TRUNK, POSTERIOR VIEW

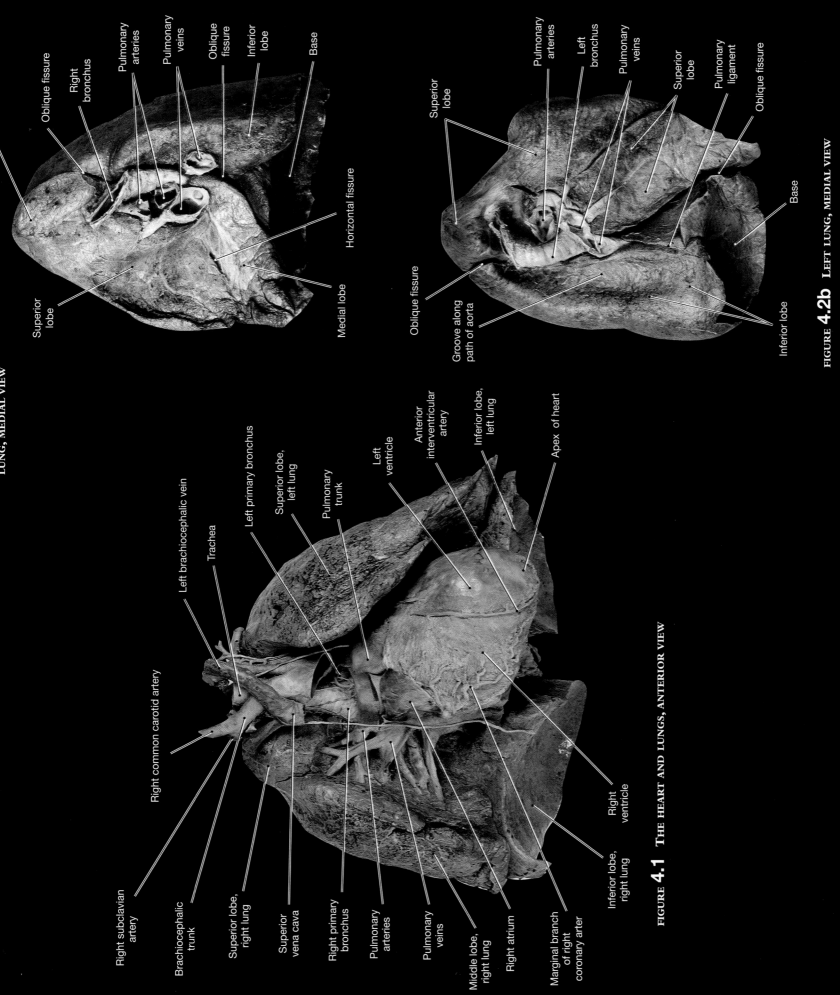

FIGURE 4.2a RIGHT
LUNG, MEDIAL VIEW

Apex

Oblique fissure

Right bronchus

Pulmonary arteries

Pulmonary veins

Oblique fissure

Inferior lobe

Base

Superior lobe

Horizontal fissure

Medial lobe

FIGURE 4.2b LEFT LUNG, MEDIAL VIEW

Superior lobe

Pulmonary arteries

Left bronchus

Pulmonary veins

Superior lobe

Pulmonary ligament

Oblique fissure

Base

Oblique fissure

Groove along path of aorta

Inferior lobe

FIGURE 4.1 THE HEART AND LUNGS, ANTERIOR VIEW

Left brachiocephalic vein

Trachea

Left primary bronchus

Superior lobe, left lung

Pulmonary trunk

Left ventricle

Anterior interventricular artery

Inferior lobe, left lung

Apex of heart

Right subclavian artery

Brachiocephalic trunk

Right common carotid artery

Superior lobe, right lung

Superior vena cava

Right primary bronchus

Pulmonary arteries

Pulmonary veins

Middle lobe, right lung

Right atrium

Marginal branch of right coronary arter

Inferior lobe, right lung

Right ventricle

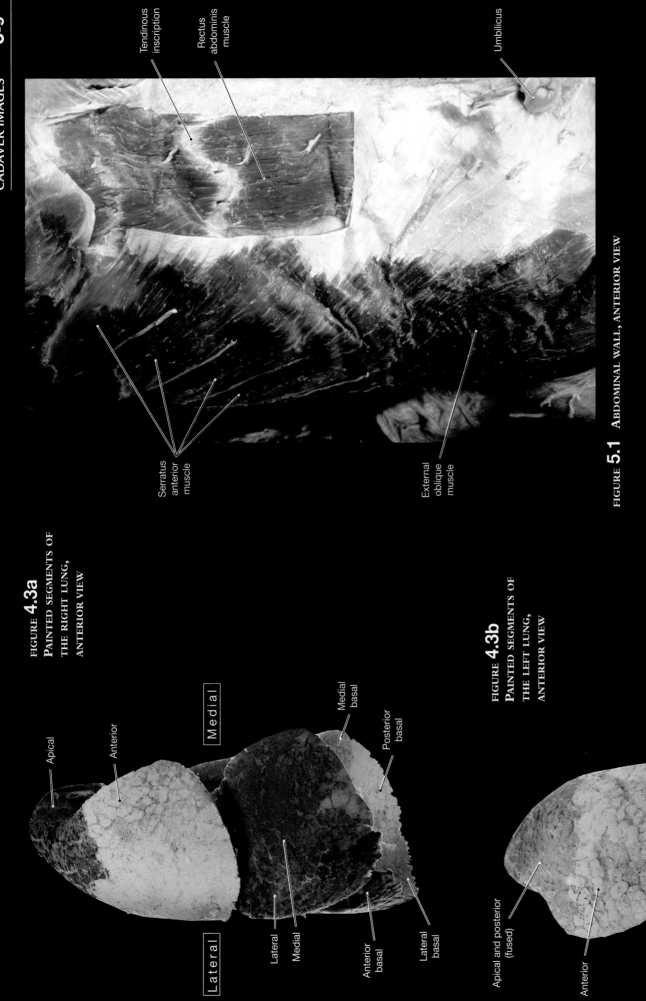

FIGURE 5.1 ABDOMINAL WALL, ANTERIOR VIEW

Tendinous inscription

Rectus abdominis muscle

Umbilicus

Serratus anterior muscle

External oblique muscle

FIGURE 4.3a
PAINTED SEGMENTS OF
THE RIGHT LUNG,
ANTERIOR VIEW

Apical

Anterior

Medial

Medial basal

Posterior basal

Lateral

Lateral

Medial

Anterior basal

Lateral basal

FIGURE 4.3b
PAINTED SEGMENTS OF
THE LEFT LUNG,
ANTERIOR VIEW

Lateral

Superior lingular

Inferior lingular

Lateral basal

Apical and posterior (fused)

Anterior

Medial

Medial basal

Posterior basal

Anterior basal

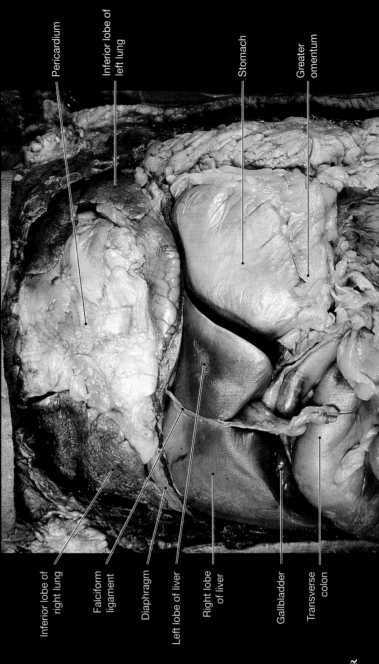

FIGURE **5.2**
ABDOMINAL MUSCLES

Pericardium

Inferior lobe of
left lung

Stomach

Greater
omentum

Inferior lobe of
right lung

Falciform
ligament

Diaphragm

Left lobe of liver

Right lobe
of liver

Gallbladder

Transverse
colon

FIGURE **5.3a**
ABDOMINAL
DISSECTION, SUPERIOR
PORTION, ANTERIOR
VIEW

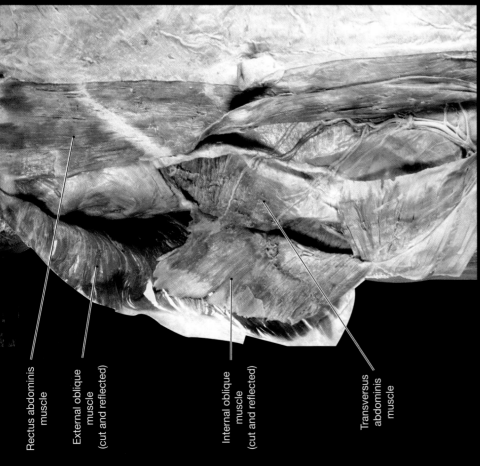

Rectus abdominis
muscle

External oblique
muscle
(cut and reflected)

Internal oblique
muscle
(cut and reflected)

Transversus
abdominis
muscle

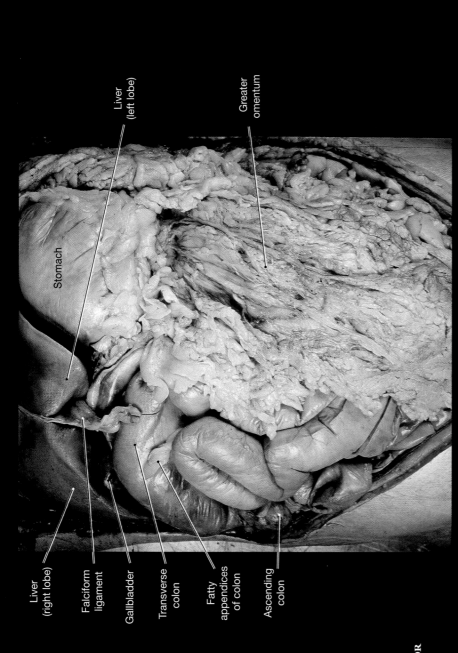

Liver
(right lobe)

Falciform
ligament

Gallbladder

Transverse
colon

Fatty
appendices
of colon

Ascending
colon

Stomach

Liver
(left lobe)

Greater
omentum

FIGURE 5.3b
ABDOMINAL
DISSECTION, INFERIOR
PORTION, ANTERIOR
VIEW

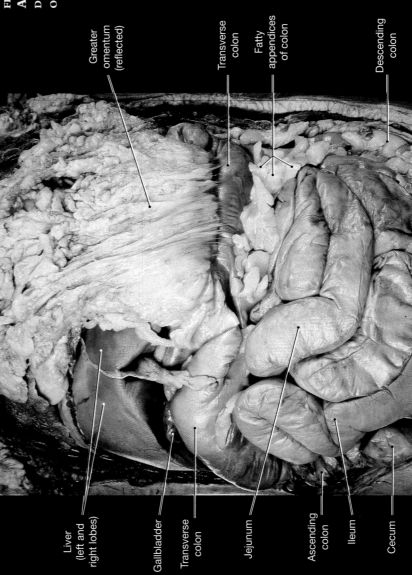

FIGURE 5.3c
ABDOMINAL
DISSECTION, GREATER
OMENTUM REFLECTED

Greater
omentum
(reflected)

Transverse
colon

Fatty
appendices
of colon

Descending
colon

Liver
(left and
right lobes)

Gallbladder

Transverse
colon

Jejunum

Ascending
colon

Ileum

Cecum

Hepatic artery

Bile duct

Common
hepatic
artery

Splenic artery

Gastroduodenal
artery

Probe in
entrance to
duodenal
papilla

Duodenum

Plicae

Stomach

Right lobe
of liver

Gallbladder

Transverse
colon

FIGURE **5.3d** ABDOMINAL DISSECTION, DUODENAL REGION

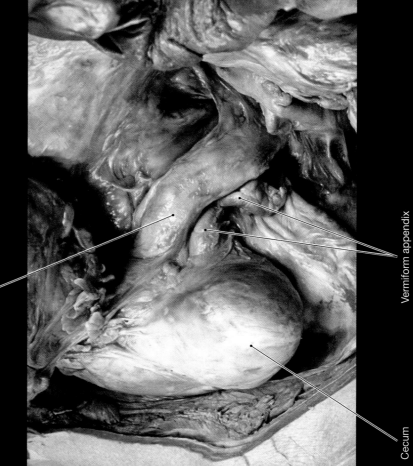

Ileum (terminal portion)

Vermiform appendix

Cecum

FIGURE **5.3e**
APPENDIX IN SITU

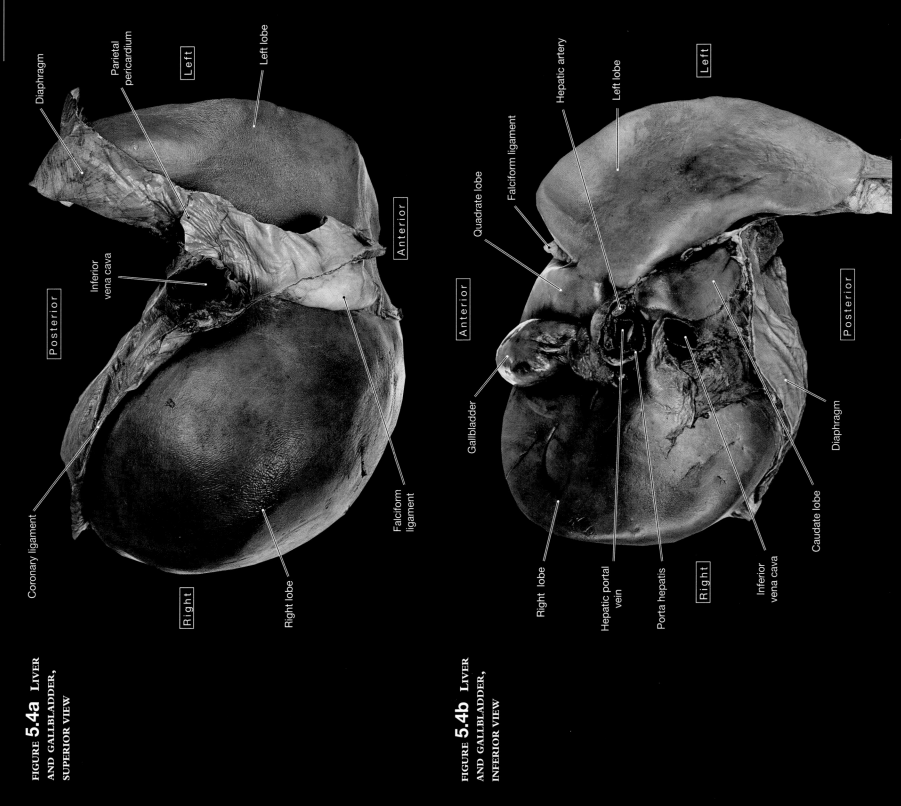

FIGURE 5.4a LIVER
AND GALLBLADDER,
SUPERIOR VIEW

Diaphragm

Parietal
pericardium

Left

Left lobe

Inferior
vena cava

Anterior

Posterior

Coronary ligament

Falciform
ligament

Right

Right lobe

FIGURE 5.4b LIVER
AND GALLBLADDER,
INFERIOR VIEW

Hepatic artery

Falciform ligament

Quadrate lobe

Left

Left lobe

Anterior

Posterior

Gallbladder

Diaphragm

Right lobe

Hepatic portal
vein

Porta hepatis

Right

Inferior
vena cava

Caudate lobe

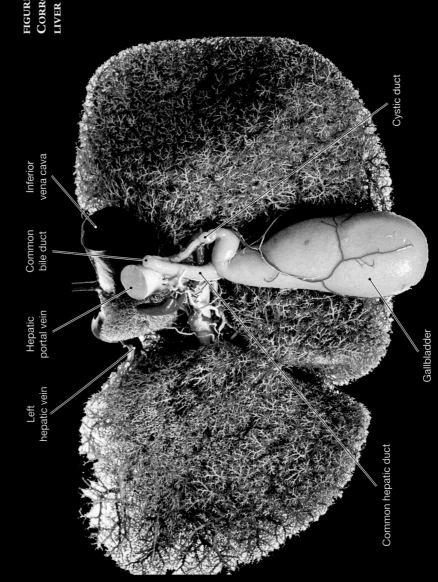

Diaphragm

Left lobe of liver

Left gastric artery

Spleen

Stomach

Left kidney

Greater omentum

Cauda equina

Falciform ligament

Cystic duct

Right lobe of liver

Gallbladder

Common bile duct

Duodenum

Pylorus

Pancreas

Transverse colon

Right kidney

Inferior vena cava

Aorta

FIGURE **5.4c** LIVER AND GALLBLADDER IN SITU

FIGURE **5.4d** CORROSION CAST OF LIVER

Inferior vena cava

Common bile duct

Hepatic portal vein

Left hepatic vein

Cystic duct

Gallbladder

Common hepatic duct

FIGURE 5.5
NORMAL AND
ABNORMAL
COLONOSCOPE

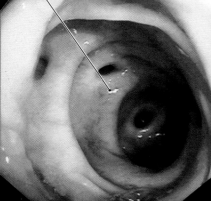

Normal section
of colon,
demonstrating
region of
previous
polyp removal.

Polyp
on wall
of colon

FIGURE 5.6a
SPLEEN, ANTERIOR
VIEW

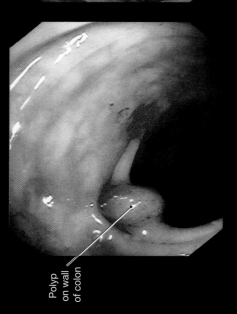

Gastric area

Spleen

Diaphragm

Stomach

Liver

Greater
omentum

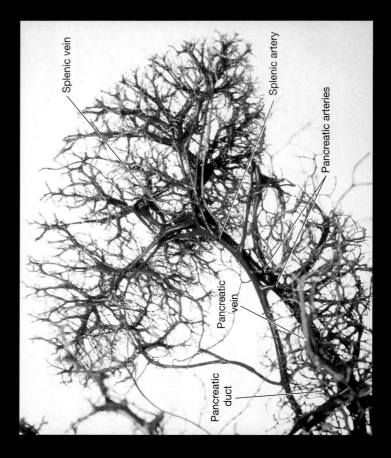

Splenic vein

Splenic artery

Pancreatic arteries

Pancreatic
vein

Pancreatic
duct

FIGURE 5.6b
CAST OF SPLENIC
AND PANCREATIC
VESSELS

FIGURE **5.7a**

SUPERIOR MESENTERIC
ARTERY

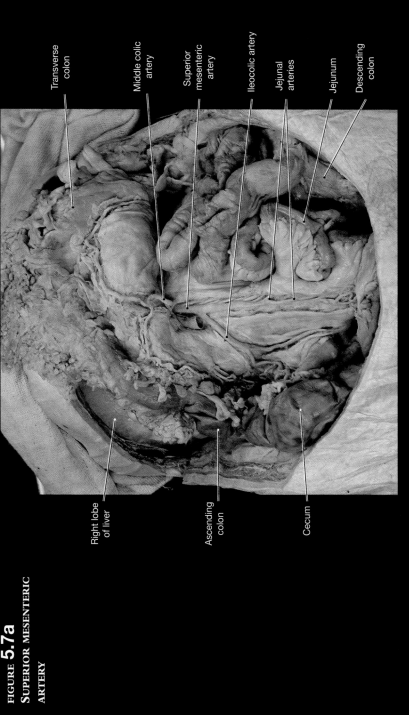

Transverse
colon

Middle colic
artery

Superior
mesenteric
artery

Ileocolic artery

Jejunal
arteries

Jejunum

Descending
colon

Right lobe
of liver

Ascending
colon

Cecum

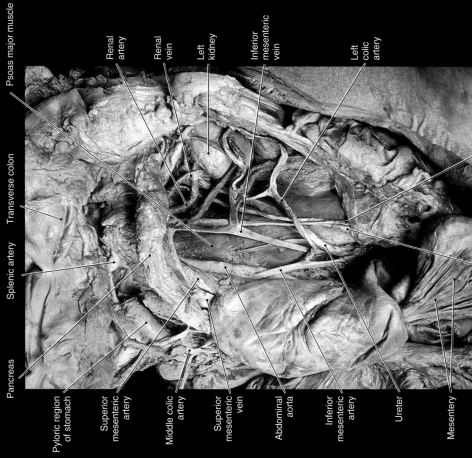

Psoas major muscle

Renal
artery

Renal
vein

Left
kidney

Inferior
mesenteric
vein

Left
colic
artery

Transverse colon

Splenic artery

Pancreas

Pyloric region
of stomach

Superior
mesenteric
artery

Middle colic
artery

Superior
mesenteric
vein

Abdominal
aorta

Inferior
mesenteric
artery

Ureter

Mesentery

FIGURE **5.7b**

INFERIOR MESENTERIC

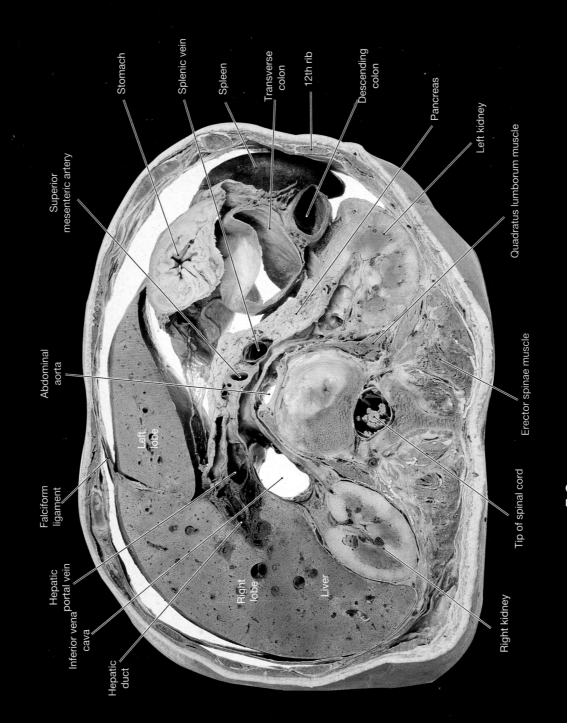

Superior
mesenteric artery

Stomach

Splenic vein

Spleen

Transverse
colon

12th rib

Descending
colon

Pancreas

Left kidney

Quadratus lumborum muscle

Abdominal
aorta

Erector spinae muscle

Left
lobe

Falciform
ligament

Hepatic
portal vein

Inferior vena
cava

Tip of spinal cord

Right
lobe

Liver

Hepatic
duct

Right kidney

FIGURE **5.8a** ABDOMINAL CAVITY, HORIZONTAL SECTION AT T_{12}

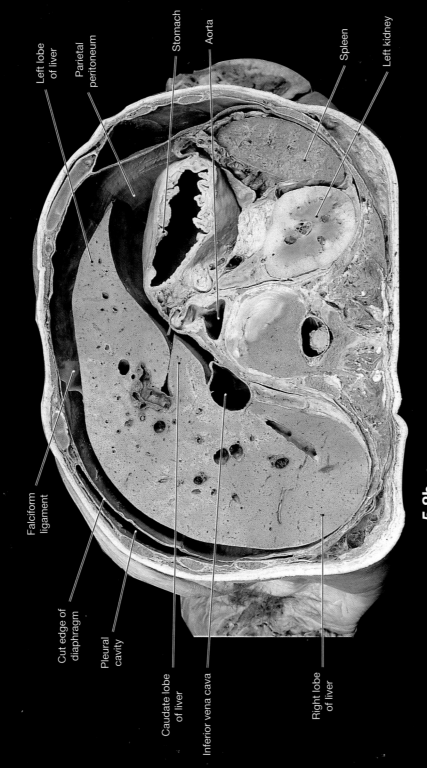

Left lobe
of liver

Parietal
peritoneum

Stomach

Aorta

Spleen

Left kidney

Falciform
ligament

Cut edge of
diaphragm

Pleural
cavity

Caudate lobe
of liver

Inferior vena cava

Right lobe
of liver

FIGURE **5.8b** ABDOMINAL CAVITY, HORIZONTAL SECTION AT L₁

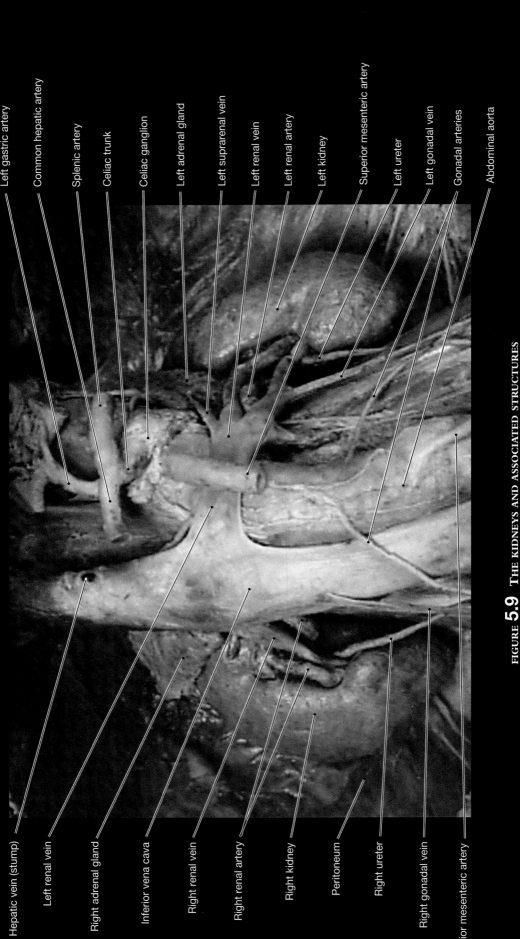

Left gastric artery

Common hepatic artery

Splenic artery

Celiac trunk

Celiac ganglion

Left adrenal gland

Left suprarenal vein

Left renal vein

Left renal artery

Left kidney

Superior mesenteric artery

Left ureter

Left gonadal vein

Gonadal arteries

Abdominal aorta

Hepatic vein (stump)

Left renal vein

Right adrenal gland

Inferior vena cava

Right renal vein

Right renal artery

Right kidney

Peritoneum

Right ureter

Right gonadal vein

ior mesenteric artery

FIGURE 5.9 THE KIDNEYS AND ASSOCIATED STRUCTURES

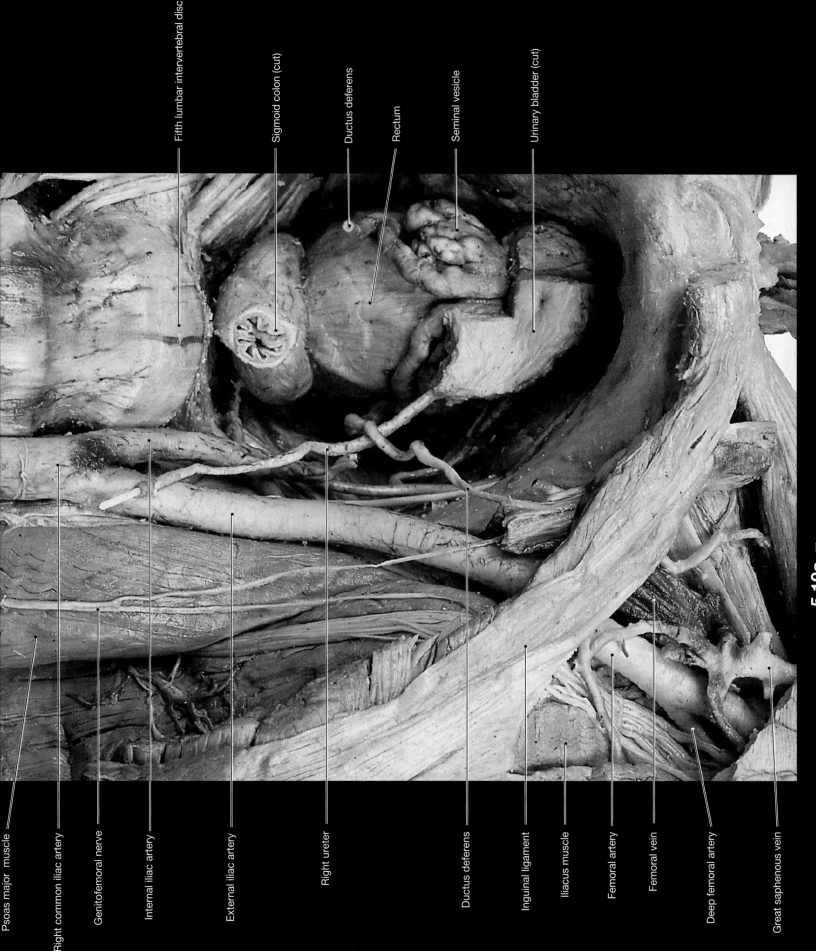

Psoas major muscle

Right common iliac artery

Genitofemoral nerve

Internal iliac artery

External iliac artery

Right ureter

Ductus deferens

Inguinal ligament

Iliacus muscle

Femoral artery

Femoral vein

Deep femoral artery

Great saphenous vein

Fifth lumbar intervertebral disc

Sigmoid colon (cut)

Ductus deferens

Rectum

Seminal vesicle

Urinary bladder (cut)

FIGURE **5.10a** THE INFERIOR PELVIS, SUPERIOR VIEW

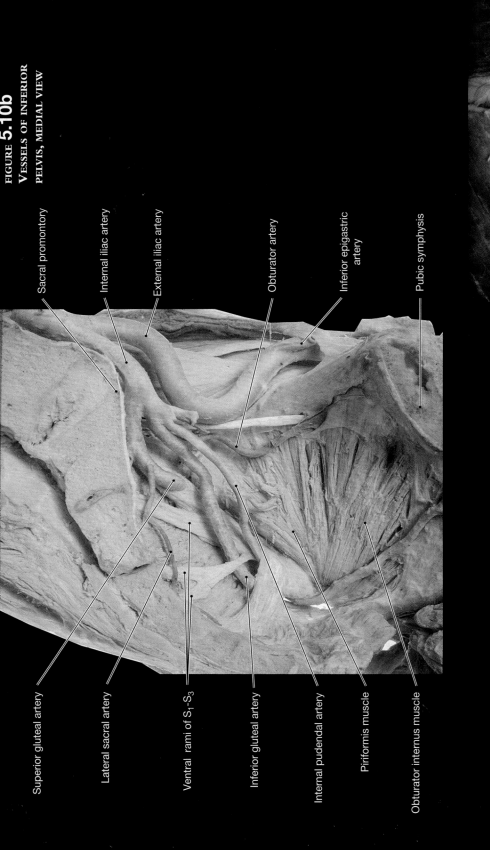

FIGURE **5.10b**
VESSELS OF INFERIOR
PELVIS, MEDIAL VIEW

Sacral promontory

Internal iliac artery

External iliac artery

Obturator artery

Inferior epigastric
artery

Pubic symphysis

Superior gluteal artery

Lateral sacral artery

Ventral rami of S_1-S_3

Inferior gluteal artery

Internal pudendal artery

Piriformis muscle

Obturator internus muscle

Rectus
abdominis
muscle

Internal
oblique muscle

Iliohypogastric
nerve

Ilioinguinal
nerve

External
oblique
aponeurosis

FIGURE **6.1** RIGHT
LOWER QUADRANT,
MALE

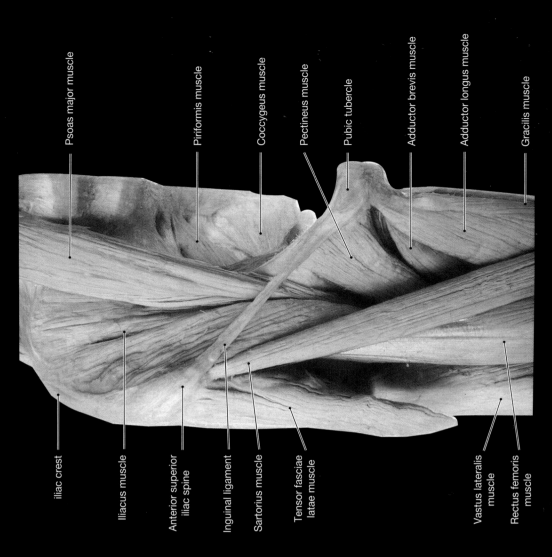

Psoas major muscle

Piriformis muscle

Coccygeus muscle

Pectineus muscle

Pubic tubercle

Adductor brevis muscle

Adductor longus muscle

Gracilis muscle

iliac crest

Iliacus muscle

Anterior superior iliac spine

Inguinal ligament

Sartorius muscle

Tensor fasciae latae muscle

Vastus lateralis muscle

Rectus femoris muscle

FIGURE 6.3 RIGHT HIP AND THIGH, ANTERIOR VIEW

FIGURE 6.2 RIGHT HIP, SUPERFICIAL DISSECTION, POSTERIOR VIEW

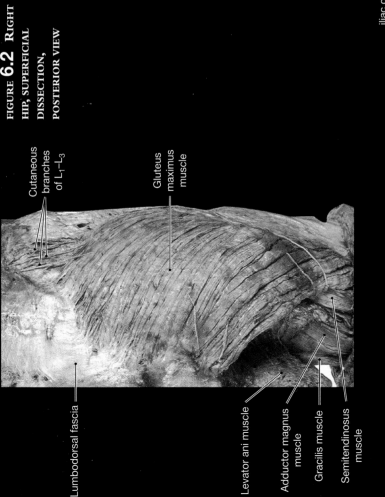

Cutaneous branches of L_1–L_3

Gluteus maximus muscle

Lumbodorsal fascia

Levator ani muscle

Adductor magnus muscle

Gracilis muscle

Semitendinosus muscle

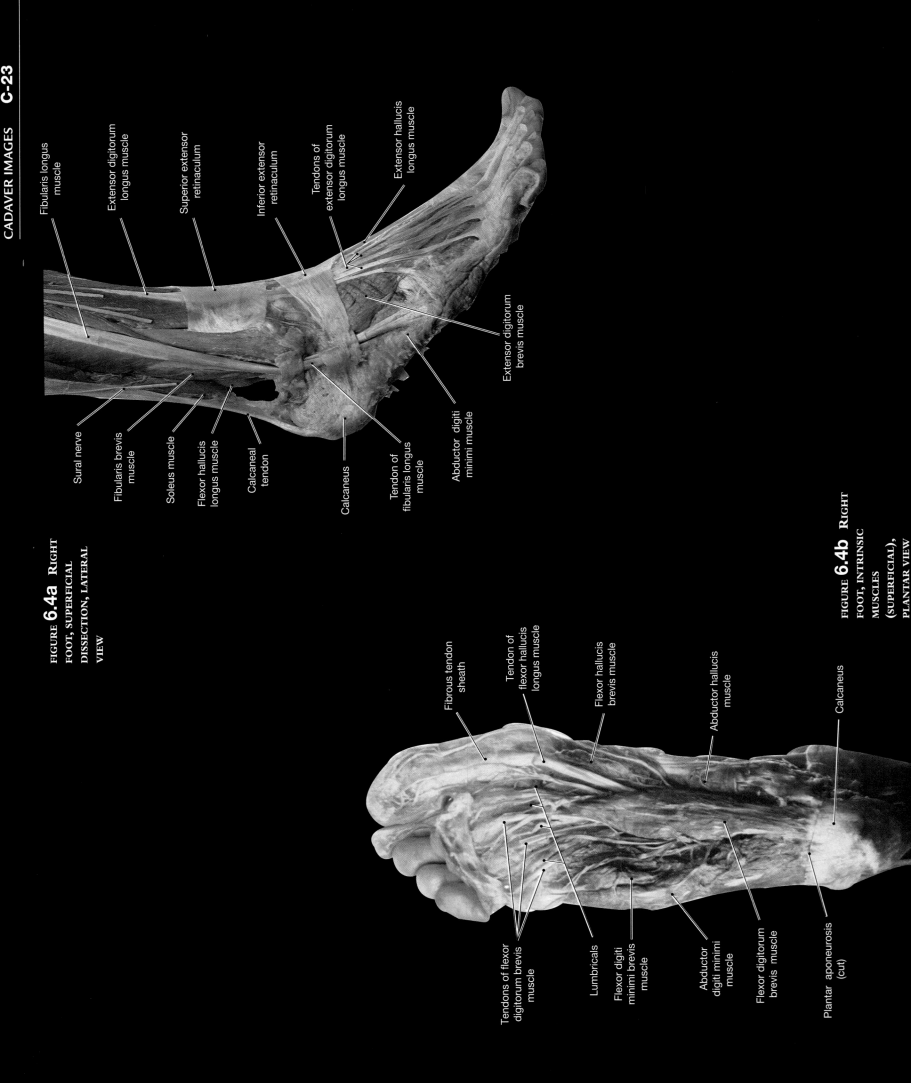

Fibularis longus muscle

Extensor digitorum longus muscle

Superior extensor retinaculum

Inferior extensor retinaculum

Tendons of extensor digitorum longus muscle

Extensor hallucis longus muscle

Extensor digitorum brevis muscle

Sural nerve

Fibularis brevis muscle

Soleus muscle

Flexor hallucis longus muscle

Calcaneal tendon

Calcaneus

Tendon of fibularis longus muscle

Abductor digiti minimi muscle

FIGURE 6.4a RIGHT FOOT, SUPERFICIAL DISSECTION, LATERAL VIEW

FIGURE 6.4b RIGHT FOOT, INTRINSIC MUSCLES (SUPERFICIAL), PLANTAR VIEW

Fibrous tendon sheath

Tendon of flexor hallucis longus muscle

Flexor hallucis brevis muscle

Abductor hallucis muscle

Calcaneus

Tendons of flexor digitorum brevis muscle

Lumbricals

Flexor digiti minimi brevis muscle

Abductor digiti minimi muscle

Flexor digitorum brevis muscle

Plantar aponeurosis (cut)

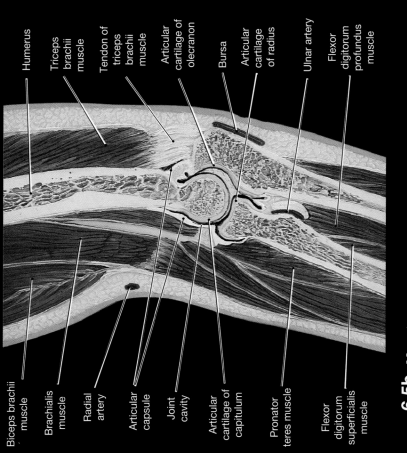
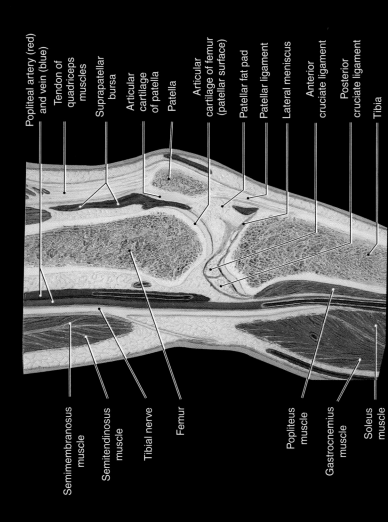

FIGURE **6.5b** MODEL OF THE ELBOW JOINT, LONGITUDINAL SECTION

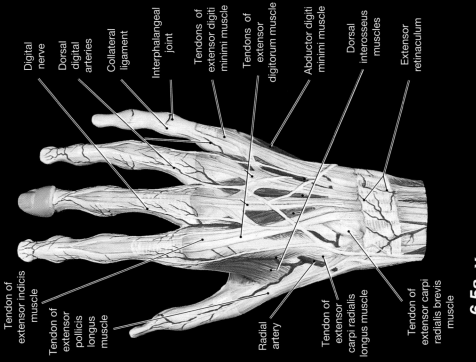

FIGURE **6.5a** MODEL OF THE RIGHT HAND, POSTERIOR VIEW

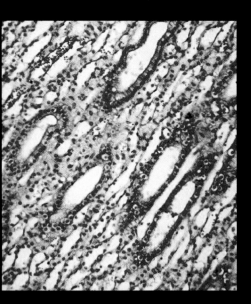

Figure 1.2 Simple cuboidal and simple squamous epithelium (LM×240)

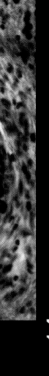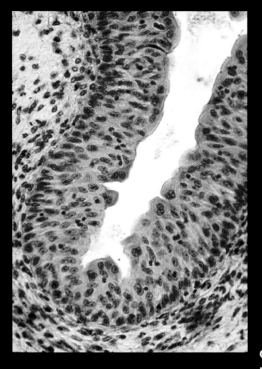

Figure 1.4 Stratified columnar epithelium (LM×480)

Figure 1.6 Transitional epithelium (urinary bladder) (LM×480)

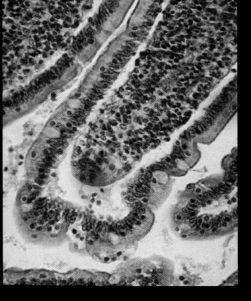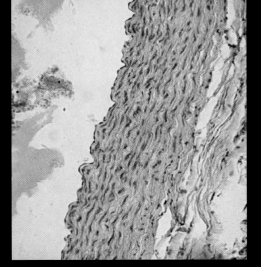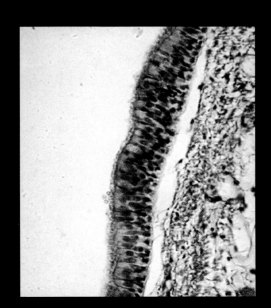

Simple columnar epithelium with goblet cells (LM×480)

Stratified squamous epithelium (LM×240)

Pseudostratified columnar epithelium (LM×480)

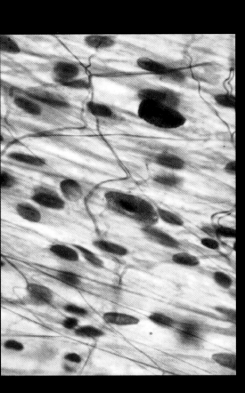

FIGURE **2.2** AREOLAR CONNECTIVE TISSUE (MESENTERIC SPREAD) (LM×480)

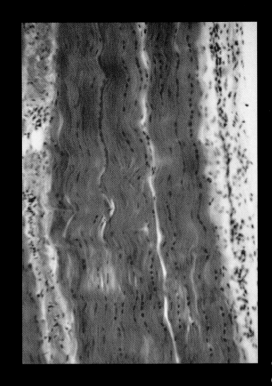

FIGURE **2.4** TENDON (DENSE REGULAR CONNECTIVE TISSUE) (LM×240)

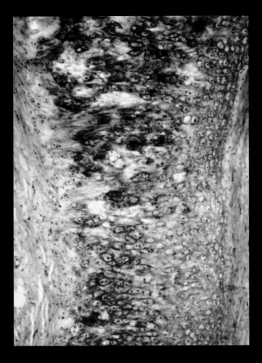

FIGURE **2.6** ELASTIC CARTILAGE (AURICLE OF THE EAR) (ELASTIN STAIN) (LM×480)

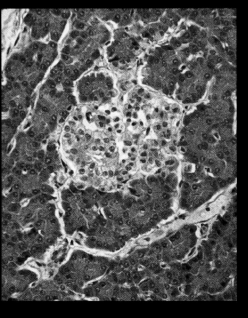

FIGURE **2.1** PANCREATIC ISLETS (ISLETS OF LANGERHANS) (LM×480)

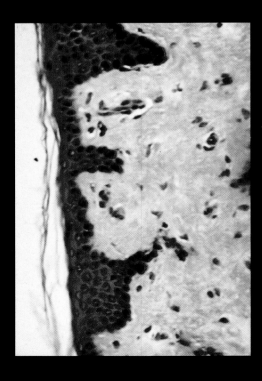

FIGURE **2.3** DENSE IRREGULAR CONNECTIVE TISSUE (DERMIS OF THE SKIN) (LM×480)

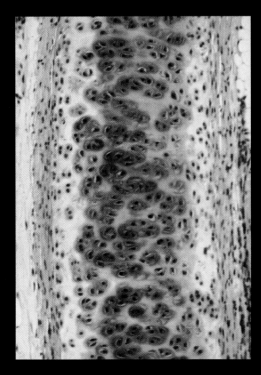

FIGURE **2.5** HYALINE CARTILAGE (TRACHEA) (LM×240)

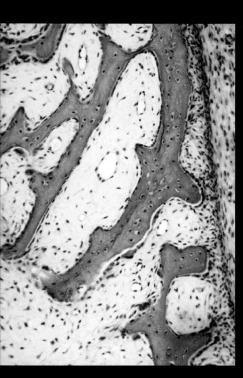

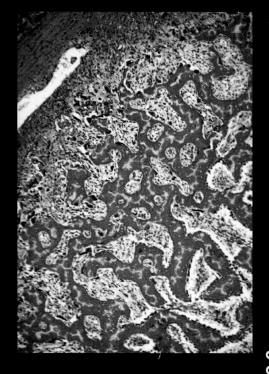

FIGURE **3.2** INTRAMEMBRANOUS (MEMBRANE) BONE DEVELOPMENT (FETAL PIG) (LM×240)

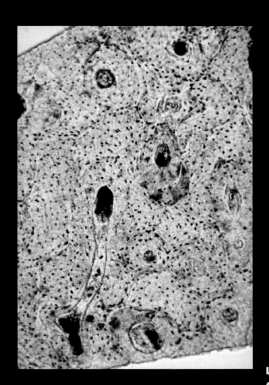

FIGURE **3.4** BONE SPICULE WITHIN THE DIAPHYSIS OF DEVELOPING BONE (LM×240)

FIGURE **3.6** TRABECULAR (CANCELLOUS) BONE (LM×240)

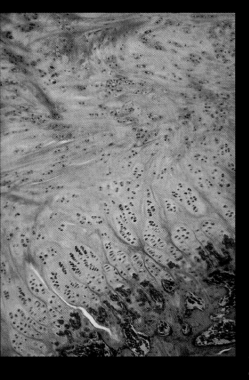

FIGURE **3.1** FIBROCARTILAGE (PUBIC SYMPHYSIS) (LM×240)

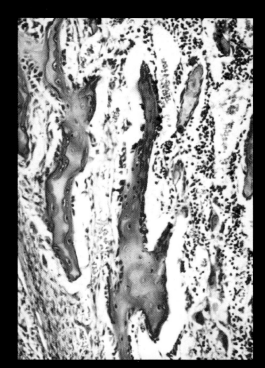

FIGURE **3.3** ENDOCHONDRAL OSSIFICATION AT THE EPIPHYSEAL CARTILAGE (FETAL METATARSAL) (LM×48)

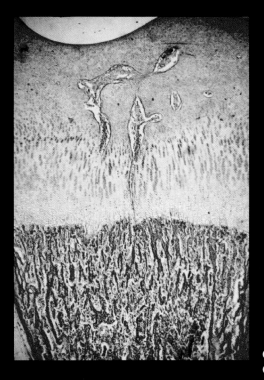

FIGURE **3.5** COMPACT BONE (CROSS-SECTION), GROUND BONE (LM×120)

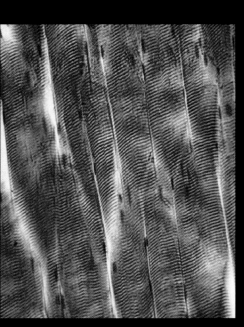

FIGURE **4.1** SKELETAL MUSCLE (CROSS SECTION) (LM×480)

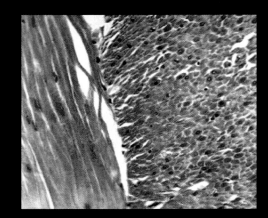

FIGURE **4.2** SKELETAL MUSCLE (LONGITUDINAL SECTION) (LM×480)

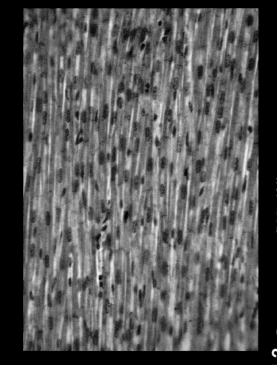

FIGURE **4.3** CARDIAC MUSCLE (LM×480)

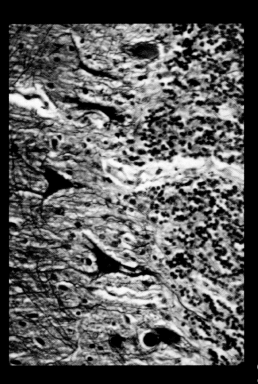

FIGURE **4.4** SMOOTH MUSCLE (LONGITUDINAL AND CROSS SECTIONS) (LM×480)

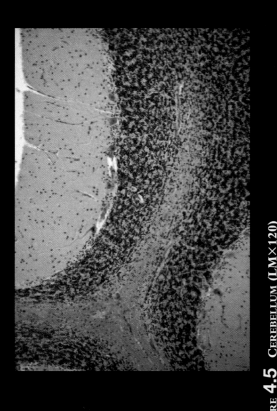

FIGURE **4.5** CEREBELLUM (LM×120)

FIGURE **4.6** PURKINJE CELLS OF THE CEREBELLUM (SILVER STAIN) (LM×480)

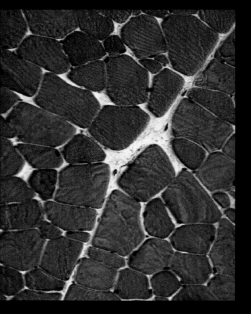

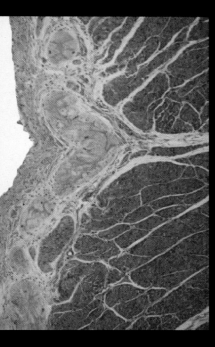

FIGURE **5.1** Peripheral nerve (cross section) (LM×110)

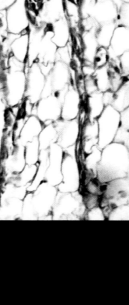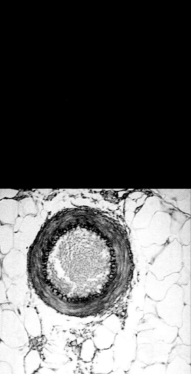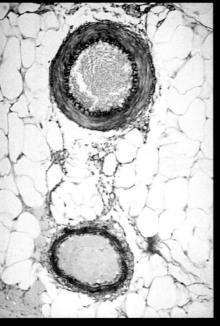

FIGURE **5.2** Purkinje fibers within ventricle of human heart (L

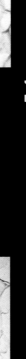

FIGURE **5.3** Cross section of artery and vein (LM×110)

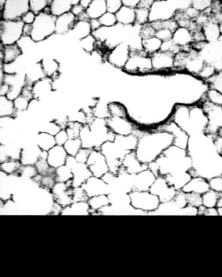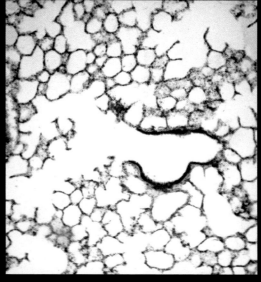

FIGURE **5.4** Capillaries within adipose tissue (LM×440)

FIGURE **5.5** Lung: transition from a terminal bronchiole to a respiratory bronchiole (LM×65)

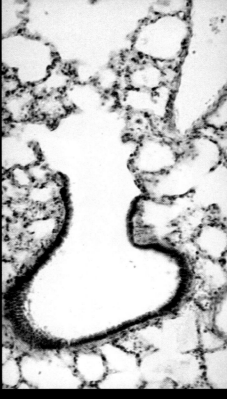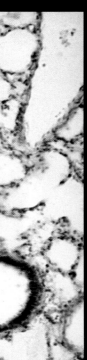

FIGURE **5.6** Lung: alveolar duct (LM×65)

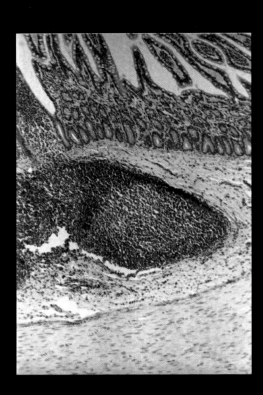

FIGURE **6.1** LUNG: PULMONARY ALVEOLI (LM×220)

FIGURE **6.2** AGGREGATED LYMPHOID NODULES (PEYER'S PATCHES) OF ILEUM (LM×120)

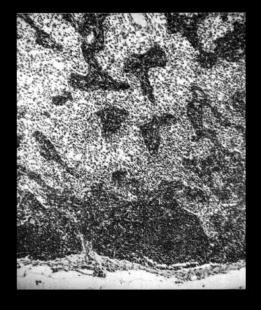

FIGURE **6.3** LYMPH NODE (LM×120)

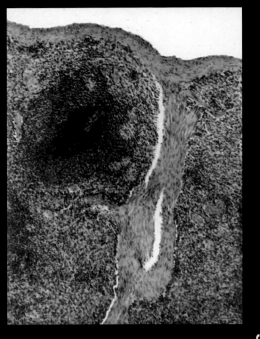

FIGURE **6.4** THYMUS OF A CHILD WITH HASSALL'S CORPUSCLES (LM×120)

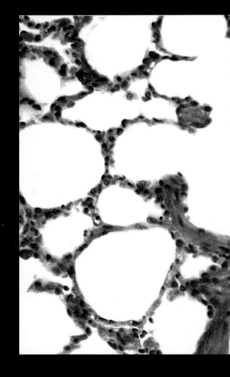

FIGURE **6.5** ATROPHIC THYMUS OF AN ADULT (LM×120)

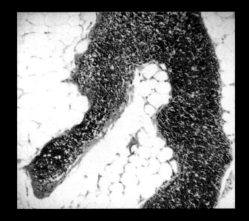

FIGURE **6.6** SPLEEN (LM×120)

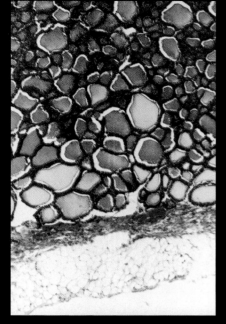

FIGURE **7.2** THYROID GLAND (LM×50)

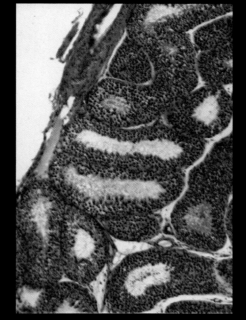

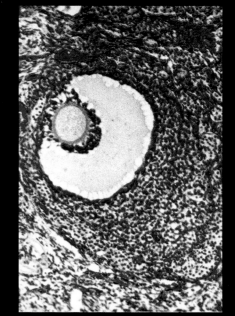

FIGURE **7.4** TESTIS (LM×50)

FIGURE **7.6** GRAAFIAN FOLLICLE WITHIN THE OVARY (LM×50)

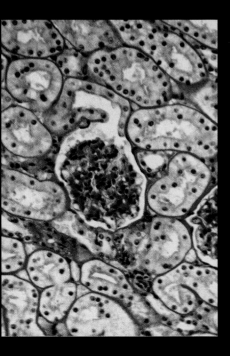

7.1 KIDNEY CORTEX: RENAL CORPUSCLE, PROXIMAL AND DISTAL CONVOLUTED TUBULES (LM×500)

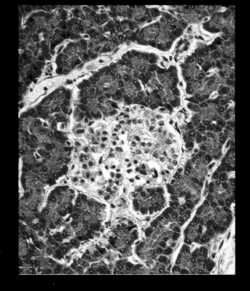

7.3 ENDOCRINE PANCREAS: PANCREATIC ISLETS (ISLETS OF LANGERHANS) (LM×200)

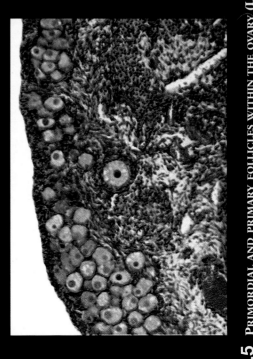

7.5 PRIMORDIAL AND PRIMARY FOLLICLES WITHIN THE OVARY (LM×50)

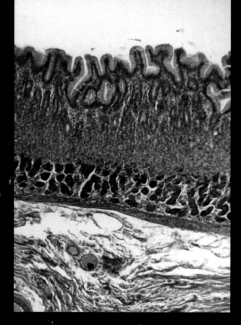

FIGURE **8.1** FUNDUS OF STOMACH (LM×50)

FIGURE **8.2** ILEUM OF SMALL INTESTINE (LM×50)

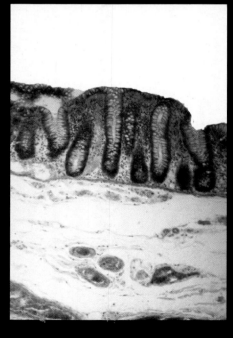

FIGURE **8.3** COLON (LM×50)

FIGURE **8.4** APPENDIX (LM×50)

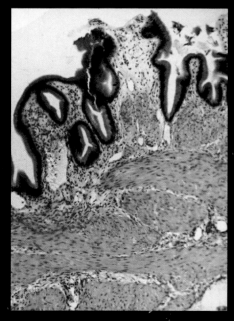

FIGURE **8.5** GALLBLADDER (LM×50)

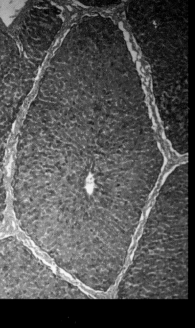

FIGURE **8.6** LIVER (LM×50)